How to Carry Water
Selected Poems of Lucille Clifton

How to Carry Water

Selected Poems of Lucille Clifton

Edited by Aracelis Girmay

american poets continuum series, no. 180

BOA Editions, Ltd. ▪ Rochester, NY ▪ 2020

First Edition
20 21 22 23 7 6 5 4 3 2

For information about permission to reuse any material from this book, please contact
The Permissions Company at www.permissionscompany.com or e-mail permdude@
gmail.com.

Publications by BOA Editions, Ltd.—a not-for-profit corporation under
section 501 (c) (3) of the United States Internal Revenue Code—are
made possible with funds from a variety of sources, including public
funds from the Literature Program of the National Endowment for the
Arts; the New York State Council on the Arts, a state agency; and the
County of Monroe, NY. Private funding sources include the Max and
Marian Farash Charitable Foundation; the Mary S. Mulligan Charitable
Trust; the Rochester Area Community Foundation; the Ames-Amzalak
Memorial Trust in memory of Henry Ames, Semon Amzalak, and Dan
Amzalak; the LGBT Fund of Greater Rochester; and contributions from many individuals
nationwide. See Colophon on page 256 for special individual acknowledgments.

Cover Design: Sandy Knight
Interior Design and Composition: Richard Foerster
BOA Logo: Mirko

BOA Editions books are available electronically through BookShare, an online distributor
offering Large-Print, Braille, Multimedia Audio Book, and Dyslexic formats, as well as
through e-readers that feature text to speech capabilities.

Library of Congress Cataloging-in-Publication Data
Names: Clifton, Lucille, 1936-2010, author. | Girmay, Aracelis, editor.
Title: How to carry water : selected poems of Lucille Clifton / edited by Aracelis Girmay.
Description: First edition. | Rochester, NY : BOA Editions, Ltd., 2020. |
  Series: American poets continuum series ; no. 180 | Includes index. |
  Summary: "A series of poems drawn from various collections published throughout the
  40-year career of American poet Lucille Clifton"— Provided by publisher.
Identifiers: LCCN 2020019710 (print) | LCCN 2020019711 (ebook) | ISBN
  9781950774142 (hardcover) | ISBN 9781950774159 (paperback) | ISBN
  9781950774166 (ebook)
Subjects: LCGFT: Poetry.
Classification: LCC PS3553.L45 H69 2020 (print) | LCC PS3553.L45 (ebook)
  | DDC 811/.54—dc23
LC record available at https://lccn.loc.gov/2020019710
LC ebook record available at https://lccn.loc.gov/2020019711

BOA Editions, Ltd.
250 North Goodman Street, Suite 306
Rochester, NY 14607
www.boaeditions.org
A. Poulin, Jr., Founder (1938–1996)

Contents

■ from **Uncollected Poems** (1973–1974)

■ from **an ordinary woman** (1974)

◼ from **quilting (1991)**

■ from **The Book of Light** (1992)

■ from **Uncollected Poems** (1993)

■ from **The Terrible Stories** (1996)

◼ from **Blessing the Boats (2000)**

◼ from **Mercy (2004)**

■ from **Voices (2008)**

■ from **Uncollected Poems (2006–2010)**

■ from **Last Poems & Drafts (2006–2010)**

■ **Previously Uncollected Poems**

foreword

1

No one writes like Lucille Clifton, and yet, if it were possible to open a voice, like a suitcase, to see what it carries inside it, I believe that inside the voices of many contemporary U.S. American poets are the poems of Lucille Clifton. There is the ferocity of her clear sight. There is the constellatory thinking where every thing is kin. The verbs of one body might also be the verbs of another seemingly disparate or distant body (her streetlights, for example, bloom). And all things have agency: as the speaker of "august the 12th" mourns a distant brother on his birthday, the speaker's hair cries, too ("my hair / is crying for her brother"). The poems, in their specificity and dilating scale, startle readers into new sense. They discomfort as often as they bless, and they bless as often as they wonder—bearing witness to joy and to struggle.

Over the course of her life, Clifton wrote 13 collections of poems, a memoir (which she worked on with her editor, Toni Morrison), and more than 16 children's books written for African American children, including *Some of the Days of Everett Anderson* and *Black BC's*. And in 1988 Clifton was the first writer to have two books of poetry nominated for the Pulitzer Prize in the same year. Those books were *Next* and *good woman*.

Her works are explicitly historical *and* of a palpable present moment. The earliest of the poems in this Selected are written during the Civil Rights Movement, the Vietnam War, the nuclear age, ecological crises, and independence movements across Africa. As the poet Kevin

Young writes in the afterword of the monumental *Collected:* "Both the poetry world and the world of the 1960s were in upheaval; the years from 1965 to 1969 saw the assassinations of Malcolm X and Martin Luther King, and the first human walking on the moon, all of which appear in the poems . . . The Black Arts movement, which Lucille Clifton found herself a part of and in many ways helped to forge, insisted on poems for and about black folks, establishing a black aesthetic based on varying ways of black speech, African structures, and political action."

Clifton's first book, *good times*, was published when her children were ages 7, 5, 4, 3, 2, and 1. Her daughters Sidney, Gillian, and Alexia remember their mother's writing as part of their daily life: "As children, we watched our mother type on her old-fashioned typewriter at the dining room table. For us, this is what mothers did; and where they did it; create worlds, play games, and share meals in the same place. Her creating space was her sanctuary, and ours. So it is with her every word." Such insistence on acknowledging all worlds in all spaces has emboldened and nourished so many of us otherwise encouraged to shutdown our truest circuitry. Instead, her poems pulse with the miracle of the porous and daily. Distilled yet capacious, her poems, like seeds, are miraculous vessels of past and future, of dense and elemental possibility. However large the story they carry, they are always scaled to the particular and resonant detail which amplifies the world at their center.

2

Lucille Clifton was born Thelma Lucille Sayles on June 27, 1936. If someone happened to have looked up at the sky that day they would have seen what looked like a moon split in half, 57% of the surface of the moon visible from the earth. I love to think of this poet born with twelve-fingers under a moon half visible, half invisible to our eyes. This poet of one eye fixed and another wandering, feeling both ordinary and magic, standing astride at least two worlds, being born out of one Thelma (her mother) into the old and new bones of her own name. Of this naming she writes:

light
on my mother's tongue
breaks through her soft
extravagant hip
into life.
lucille
she calls the light,
which was the name
of the grandmother
who waited by the crossroads
in virginia
and shot the whiteman off his horse,
killing the killer of sons.
light breaks from her life
to her lives . . .

mine already is
an afrikan name.

Her poem reveals an archive of, among other things, some of what
African America does to English and some of what English does to
African America. In the memoir *Generations* she writes this of her
lineage:

> And Lucy was hanged. Was hanged, the lady whose
> name they gave me like a gift had her neck pulled up by
> a rope until the neck broke and I can see Mammy Ca'line
> standing straight as a soldier in green Virginia [...] and
> I know that her child made no sound and I turn in my
> chair and arch my back and make this sound for my two
> mothers and for all Dahomey women.

Such repetitions of names and stories move across her work. Histories
written in circles much like time and weather are recorded in the rings
of a tree. It was toward such repetitions and echoes that I listened,
and out of them I began to see the shape of this Selected of poems
rendered with documentary, spiritual, and mystical sensibilities.

Peter Conners, my editor and the publisher of BOA Editions, calls it "listening for Ms. Lucille." I tried to listen so close I even dreamed of her voice one January morning. It seems not mine to keep but something I should share with you: *You're always whole*, she said. *Except when you're dreaming you're a quarter open.*

3

I tried to walk back through the final selections open as I'd be in a dream, or toward that kind of openness anyway. I listened for what I understood to be repeated resonances and reckonings across her life—the power of words, the loss of her mother, the deaths of the beloveds, the poem as a way to wonder, wonder as a way to live. Abortions. Children. The magic of hands. The violations of hands. Environmental crises and the links between racial violence and the devastation of the environment. The terrible stories of the terrible things we do to one another. I listened and heard something mystical: "the light flaring/ behind what has been called / the world . . ." I listened for what was strange and mysterious and a quarter open. I listened for what was sharp, clear, and yet prismatic and complex. I heard her, again and again, claim her Ones as the ones in the ground without headstones, the ones ringing like black bells, Black people, Black women people. Clifton says:

> study the masters
>
> like my aunt timmie.
> it was her iron,
> or one like hers,
> that smoothed the sheets...

Part of her brilliance is in her ability to name, with specificity, her kin, while also leaving an opening for those outside of the frame of her particular knowing. The words "like" and "or" anchor us in the concrete while pointing us to a knowledge still outside of the poem.

4

How to Carry Water begins with the poem "5/23/67 R.I.P." Written in '67 it was not published until 2012, in *The Collected*. I give deep and abiding thanks to editors Kevin Young and Michael Glaser for the hours and devotion which brought that collection into the world, and out of which this Selected emerges.

In "5/23/67 R.I.P." Clifton mourns the loss of the Great Langston Hughes, writer, activist, and chronicler of Black Life. The poem, dated one day after his death, closes with a lament ("Oh who gone remember now like it was . . .") but in the lines directly above I come to understand that his death also marks Clifton's eye as she reads even the moon through the veil of her own mourning:

> make the moon look like
> a yellow man in a veil
> watching the troubled people
> running and crying
> > Oh who gone remember now like it was,
> > Langston gone.

The poem is an attempt to remember a community's loss while simultaneously marking the impossibility of that record ever being precise enough. The decision to begin the Selected here carried a few hopes. I wanted to mark Clifton's documentary sensibility and a strange, triple-eyed imagery where the moon, for example, looks like a yellow man in a veil, a mourner among mourners, but also watching, like, maybe, a poet. A poet like Langston, a poet like Ms. Lucille.

5

The Selected begins with "5/23/67 R.I.P." and moves chronologically across the work ending with ten previously uncollected poems. Most of these poems my sister-poet Kamilah Aisha Moon and I came upon together while visiting Clifton's papers at Emory. To see those poems whose margins were sometimes scribbled with the math of bills and the drawings of children, was to have yet another sense of the hours and breaths by which the poems were made. And to read across her revisions was to also sense the circuitry and pull of her own listening. In "Poem With Rhyme," for example, she changes: "I have cried, me and my / possible yes . . ." to "I have cried, me and my / black yes . . ." This change from "possible" to "black" to me revealed a circuitry of association. For Clifton the lineage of "black" is a lineage of possibility.

I revisited those poems again and again to see which, if any, might resonate with the other poems I'd already set aside for the Selected. A few of them, yes, seemed to utterly be a part and so I contacted the publisher and Clifton's daughters. Now these are the last poems of the book. This said, it is not clear to me when these poems were written. I love that an otherwise chronological organization is troubled by these poems I cannot place in order or time definitively. This, too, seems essential and part of what her work offers. This, too, seems part of what I have been listening for.

6

In the archives I also found what I'd been looking for. I knew that Toni Morrison was Clifton's editor at Random House when Clifton was writing *Generations*. I had been hoping to find correspondence between them about the writing, perhaps just as a way of hearing these wondrous and brilliant writers thinking together generally, but I also hoped to understand something about each of their poetics.

In May of 1972, Toni Morrison writes to Lucille Clifton thanking her for agreeing to read stories by Toni Cade Bambara. She writes: "I think they are stunning—and hope you will too." When Toni Cade Bambara's *Gorilla, My Love* was published in 1972, Clifton's words were published on the back: "She has captured it all, how we really talk... She must love us very much." (So here we see that for Clifton, precision and love hold each other.) In November of 1973 Morrison again writes to Clifton, New York to Baltimore: "So good to meet you at last. I wish we had more time—I had just discovered what it was when the time was gone. Come back."

Later in the letter Morrison shares her notes on Clifton's manuscript— questions about titles and diction, a suggestion to delete a last line here and a fourth verse there. In the margins of Morrison's letter are Clifton's handwritten marks, clear and to the point:

2. a. I don't agree. "precious" and "valuable" are different.
   b. I agree about Sunflowers, suggest we leave it out . . .
   c. I don't agree.
   d. I agree. That fourth verse belongs in my memory not in the poem.
   e. I want/mean to say this. It needs saying. again.
   f. I don't agree.
   g. I don't agree.
   h. I agree.

What do you think about what I think?

Love to yourself and
your boys,
Lucille

7

water sign woman

the woman who feels everything
sits in her new house
waiting for someone to come
who knows how to carry water
without spilling, who knows
why the desert is sprinkled
with salt, why tomorrow
is such a long and ominous word.

they say to the feel things woman
that little she dreams is possible,
that there is only so much
joy to go around, only so much

water. there are no questions
for this, no arguments. she has

to forget to remember the edge
of the sea, they say, to forget . . .

In "Uses of the Erotic" (1978) Audre Lorde writes: "There are many
kinds of power, used and unused, acknowledged or otherwise. The
erotic is a resource within each of us that lies in a deeply female and
spiritual plane, firmly rooted in the power of our unexpressed or
unrecognized feeling. In order to perpetuate itself, every oppression
must corrupt or distort those various sources of power within the
culture of the oppressed that can provide energy for change." And
later: "Another important way in which the erotic connection func-
tions is the open and fearless underlining of my capacity for joy." In
articulating the power of the erotic as, among other things, something
by which we can gauge our feelings and sense of fulfillment, Lorde
also articulates a relationship between the erotic and attention: "Our
erotic knowledge empowers us, becomes a lens through which we
scrutinize all aspects of our existence, forcing us to evaluate those
aspects honestly in terms of their relative meaning within our lives."

I read a thread from dreams to joy to water to Lorde's erotic. I read
a verse that does not abide by the forgetting that others want this
water woman to abide. In the waters of this poem swirls another of
her poems:

why some people be mad at me sometimes

they ask me to remember
but they want me to remember
their memories
and i keep on remembering
mine.

So then what is water? What can it be?

The element. Daily, ordinary, enduring. Extraordinary, shiftful, expansive. A word for what one is thirsty for. Desire. What can quench. What can be swum and what cannot be swum. The Atlantic. Middle Passages. The distance between this and that. That which cannot be held for long in bare hands but can be carried. The sky, the river, the rain. Knowing and unknowing. Ancestral. Elder, our singular and plural and going on.

8 *I am building a ladder of listening*
I was listening for Ms. Lucille. And in that listening I was lucky to be in conversation with several writers. Such exchanges added to my thinking, especially an early conversation with Sidney Clifton about desire in her mother's poems. Desire led me to "water sign woman" and to the waiting, knowing, and feeling there.

9
I walked awake and differently attentive to the bridge between Clifton's poems and the lives of those around me. Just days after coming to *How to Carry Water* as the title, for example, I sat reading the big, black *Collected* in the café below my apartment. The young waiter saw the book and said, *Oh my god! I love Lucille Clifton's poetry!* He talked about "homage to my hips" and how she talks about things he didn't think of as being in poems. Before leaving I said it was so nice to meet him and asked him his name. He said, *River.* And I thought, Of course!

I listened to the songs that Ms. Lucille's daughters told me she loved, among them: Ray Charles' "Georgia On My Mind," "Hit the Road, Jack," "Born to Lose," and "America the Beautiful." Aretha's *Aretha Arrives* and *Aretha's Gold.* The songs of Joe Cocker, Dionne Warwick, Nina Simone. Creedence Clearwater Revival singing *I wanna know, have you ever seen the rain . . .*

10 *a ladder of listening*
When I asked Sonia Sanchez about what she hoped for this Selected, she spoke about an old-fashioned smile that people sometimes get

when they hear Lucille Clifton's name. She said, in a way that infused each word with a sense of looking forward and looking back: "I want Lucille to be seen, not an old-fashioned smile." And she spoke about how difficult so many of Clifton's poems are, especially the poems about her father sexually abusing her. She spoke of how political her poems, and how discomforting and fierce that work. And what that took.

She said resoundingly: "This was a brilliant woman."

11
. . . and I turn in my chair and arch my back and make this sound for my two mothers and for all Dahomey women.

12
Come back. It is the "Come back" of Toni Morrison's letter that I keep hearing. It was written in 1973 but catches so sharply still, in the light. And yet this is also true:

> in populated air
> our ancestors continue.
> i have seen them.
> i have heard
> their shimmering voices
> singing.

—aracelis girmay
Brooklyn, NY
2020

How to Carry Water

5/23/67

R.I.P.

The house that is on fire
pieces all across the sky
make the moon look like
a yellow man in a veil
watching the troubled people
running and crying
    Oh who gone remember now like it was,
    Langston gone.

■

SPRING THOUGHT FOR THELMA

Someone who had her fingers
set for growing,
settles into garden.
If old desires linger
she will be going
flower soon. Pardon
her little blooms
whose blossoming was stunted
by rooms.

■

Everytime i talk about
the old folks
tomming and easying their way
happy with their nothing and
grateful for their sometime
i run up against my old black
Mama
and i shut up and stand there
shamed.

■

a poem written for many moynihans

ignoring me
you turn into blind alleys
follow them around
to your boyhouse
meet your mother
green in her garden
kiss what she holds out to you
her widowed arm and
this is betterness

ignoring me
you make a brother for you
she drops him in the pattern
you made when you were sonning
you name her wife to keep her
and this is betterness

ignoring me
your days slide into seasons
you build a hole to fall in
and send your brother running
following blind alleys
turning white as winter
and this is
betterness

∎

the poet is thirty two

she has such knowledges as
rats have,
the sound of cat
the smell of cheese
where the holes are,
she is comfortable
hugging the walls
she trembles over herself
in the light
and she will leave disaster
when she can.

■

take somebody like me
who Daddy took to sunday school
and who was a member of the choir
and helped with the little kids at
the church picnic,
deep into Love thy Neighbor   take
somebody like me
who cried at the March on Washington
and thought Pennsylvania was beautiful
let her read a lot
let her notice things
then
hit her with the Draft Riots and the
burning of the colored orphan asylum
and the children in the church and
the Lamar busses and
the assassinations and the
bombs and all the spittings on our
children and
these beasts were not niggers
these beasts were not niggers
she
will be too old to change and
she will not hate consistently   or long
and she will know herself a coward and
a fool.

■

my mama moved among the days
like a dreamwalker in a field;
seemed like what she touched was hers
seemed like what touched her couldn't hold,
she got us almost through the high grass
then seemed like she turned around and ran
right back in
right back on in

■

miss rosie

when i watch you
wrapped up like garbage
sitting, surrounded by the smell
of too old potato peels
or
when i watch you
in your old man's shoes
with the little toe cut out
sitting, waiting for your mind
like next week's grocery
i say
when i watch you
you wet brown bag of a woman
who used to be the best looking gal in georgia
used to be called the Georgia Rose
i stand up
through your destruction
i stand up

■

the 1st

what i remember about that day
is boxes stacked across the walk
and couch springs curling through the air
and drawers and tables balanced on the curb
and us, hollering,
leaping up and around
happy to have a playground;

nothing about the emptied rooms
nothing about the emptied family

■

running across to the lot
in the middle of the cement days
to watch the big boys trembling
as the dice made poets of them
if we remembered to despair
i forget

i forget
while the streetlights were blooming
and the sharp birdcall
of the iceman and his son
and the ointment of the ragman's horse
sang spring
our fathers were dead and
our brothers were dying

■

if i stand in my window
naked in my own house
and press my breasts
against my windowpane
like black birds pushing against glass
because i am somebody
in a New Thing

and if the man come to stop me
in my own house
naked in my own window
saying i have offended him
i have offended his

Gods

let him watch my black body
push against my own glass
let him discover self
let him run naked through the streets
crying
praying in tongues

■

for deLawd

people say they have a hard time
understanding how i
go on about my business
playing my ray charles
hollering at the kids—
seem like my afro
cut off in some old image
would show i got a long memory
and i come from a line
of black and going on women
who got used to making it through murdered sons
and who grief kept on pushing
who fried chicken
ironed
swept off the back steps
who grief kept
for their still alive sons
for their sons coming
for their sons gone
just pushing

■

ca'line's prayer

i have got old
in a desert country
i am dry
and black as drought
don't make water
only acid
even dogs won't drink

remember me from wydah
remember the child
running across dahomey
black as ripe papaya
juicy as sweet berries
and set me in the rivers of your glory

Ye Ma Jah

■

generations

people who are going to be
in a few years
bottoms of trees
bear a responsibility to something
besides people
          if it was only
you and me
sharing the consequences
it would be different
it would be just
generations of men
          but
this business of war
these war kinds of things
are erasing those natural
obedient generations
who ignored pride
          stood on no hind legs
          begged no water
          stole no bread
did their own things

and the generations of rice
of coal
of grasshoppers

by their invisibility
denounce us

■

flowers

here we are
running with the weeds
colors exaggerated
pistils wild
embarrassing the calm family flowers   oh
here we are
flourishing for the field
and the name of the place
is Love

■

after kent state

only to keep
his little fear
he kills his cities
and his trees
even his children   oh
people
white ways are
the way of death
come into the
black
and live

■

being property once myself
i have a feeling for it,
that's why i can talk
about environment.
what wants to be a tree,
ought to be he can be it.
same thing for other things.
same thing for men.

■

the lost baby poem

the time i dropped your almost body down
down to meet the waters under the city
and run one with the sewage to the sea
what did i know about waters rushing back
what did i know about drowning
or being drowned

you would have been born in winter
in the year of the disconnected gas
and no car   we would have made the thin
walk over genesee hill into the canada wind
to watch you slip like ice into strangers' hands
you would have fallen naked as snow into winter
if you were here i could tell you these
and some other things

if i am ever less than a mountain
for your definite brothers and sisters
let the rivers pour over my head
let the sea take me for a spiller
of seas   let black men call me stranger
always   for your never named sake

■

apology

(to the panthers)

i became a woman
during the old prayers
among the ones who wore
bleaching cream to bed
and all my lessons stayed

i was obedient
but brothers i thank you
for these mannish days

i remember again the wise one
old and telling of suicides
refusing to be slaves

i had forgotten and
brothers i thank you
i praise you
i grieve my whiteful ways

■

lately
everybody i meet
is a poet.

"Look here"

said the tall delivery man
who is always drunk

"whoever can do better
ought to do it. Me,
I'm 25 years old
and all the white boys
my age
are younger than me."

so saying
he dropped a six pack
turned into most of my cousins
and left.

■

listen children
keep this in the place
you have for keeping
always
keep it all ways

we have never hated black

listen
we have been ashamed
hopeless   tired   mad
but always
all ways
we loved us

we have always loved each other
children   all ways

pass it on

■

the news

everything changes   the old
songs click like light bulbs
going off   the faces
of men dying scar the air
the moon becomes the mountain
who would have thought
who would believe
dead things could stumble back
and kill us

■

the bodies broken on
the trail of tears
and the bodies melted
in middle passage
are married to rock and
ocean by now
and the mountains crumbling on
white men
the waters pulling white men down
sing for red dust and black clay
good news about the earth

■

song

sons of slaves and
daughters of masters
all come up from the
ocean together

daughters of slaves and
sons of masters
all ride out on the
empty air

brides and hogs and dogs and babies
close their eyes against the sight

bricks and sticks and diamonds witness
a life of death is the death of life

■

africa

home
oh
home
the soul of your
variety
all of my bones
remember

■

earth

here is where it was dry
when it rained
and also
here
under the same
what was called
tree
it bore varicolored
flowers   children   bees
all this used to be a
place once   all this
was a nice place
once

■

God send easter

and we will lace the
jungle on
and step out
brilliant as birds
against the concrete country
feathers waving as we
dance toward jesus
sun reflecting mango
and apple as we
glory in our skin

■

so close
they come so close
to being beautiful
if they had hung on
maybe five more years
we would have been together
for these new things
and for them old niggers
to have come so close   oh
seem like some black people
missed out even more than
all the time

■

poem for my sisters

like he always said
        the things of daddy
        will find him
        leg to leg and
        lung to lung
        and the man who
        killed the bear
        so we could cross the mountain
        will cross it whole
        and holy
"all goodby ain't gone"

■

Phillis Wheatley Poetry Festival

November 1973

for Margaret Walker Alexander

I
Hey Nikki
wasn't it good, wasn't it good June
Carole wasn't it good, wasn't it good Alice
Carolyn wasn't it good, Audre wasn't it good
wasn't it good Sonia, sister wasn't it good?

Wasn't it good Margaret, wasn't it good?
Wasn't it good Linda, Mari wasn't it good
wasn't it good Margaret, wasn't it good Naomi
wasn't it good Sarah, sister wasn't it good?

Hey Gloria, Jobari wasn't it good?
Wasn't it good Malaika, wasn't it good?
Wasn't it good sister, wasn't it good sister,
Sister, sisters, sisters, oh sisters,
oh ain't it good?

II
What Nikki knows

Jesus Keep Me is
what kept me and
How I Got Over is
how we got over.

III
to Margaret and Gwen

Mama
two dozen daughters stand together
holding hands and singing cause
you such a good mama we
got to be good girls.

■

in salem
to jeanette

weird sister
the black witches know that
the terror is not in the moon
choreographing the dance of wereladies
and the terror is not in the broom
swinging around to the hum of cat music
nor the wild clock face grinning from the wall,
the terror is in the plain pink
at the window
and the hedges moral as fire
and the plain face of the white woman watching us
as she beats her ordinary bread.

■

salt

for sj and jj

he is as salt
to her,
a strange sweet
a peculiar money
precious and valuable
only to her tribe,
and she is salt
to him,
something that rubs raw
that leaves a tearful taste
but what he will
strain the ocean for and
what he needs.

■

new bones

we will wear
new bones again.
we will leave
these rainy days,
break out through
another mouth
into sun and honey time.
worlds buzz over us like bees,
we be splendid in new bones.
other people think they know
how long life is
how strong life is.
we know.

■

harriet
if i be you
let me not forget
to be the pistol
pointed
to be the madwoman
at the rivers edge
warning
be free or die
and isabell
if i be you
let me in my
sojourning
not forget
to ask my brothers
ain't i a woman too
and
grandmother
if i be you
let me not forget to
work hard
trust the Gods
love my children and
wait.

■

roots

call it our craziness even,
call it anything.
it is the life thing in us
that will not let us die.
even in death's hand
we fold the fingers up
and call them greens and
grow on them,
we hum them and make music.
call it our wildness then,
we are lost from the field
of flowers, we become
a field of flowers.
call it our craziness
our wildness
call it our roots,
it is the light in us
it is the light of us
it is the light, call it
whatever you have to,
call it anything.

■

to ms. ann

i will have to forget
your face
when you watched me breaking
in the fields,
missing my children.

i will have to forget
your face
when you watched me carry
your husband's
stagnant water.

i will have to forget
your face
when you handed me
your house
to make a home,

and you never called me sister
then, you never called me sister
and it has only been forever and
i will have to forget your face.

■

last note to my girls

for sid, rica, gilly and neen

my girls
my girls
my almost me
mellowed in a brown bag
held tight and straining
at the top
like a good lunch
until the bag turned weak and wet
and burst in our honeymoon rooms.
we wiped the mess and
dressed you in our name and
here you are
my girls
my girls
forty quick fingers
reaching for the door.

i command you to be
good runners
to go with grace
go well in the dark and
make for high ground
my dearest girls
my girls
my more than me.

■

a visit to gettysburg

i will
touch stone
yes i will
teach white rock to answer
yes i will
walk in the wake
of the battle sir
while the hills
and the trees
and the guns watch me
a touchstone
and i will rub
"where is my black blood
and black bone?"
and the grounds
and the graves
will throw off they clothes
and touch stone
for this touchstone.

■

this morning
(for the girls of eastern high school)

this morning
this morning
          i met myself
coming in

a bright
jungle girl
shining
quick as a snake
a tall
tree girl a
me girl
          i met myself
this morning
coming in

and all day
i have been
a black bell
ringing
i survive
        survive
survive

■

the lesson of the falling leaves

the leaves believe
such letting go is love
such love is faith
such faith is grace
such grace is god
i agree with the leaves

■

i am running into a new year
and the old years blow back
like a wind
that i catch in my hair
like strong fingers like
all my old promises and
it will be hard to let go
of what i said to myself
about myself
when i was sixteen and
twentysix and thirtysix
even thirtysix but
i am running into a new year
and i beg what i love and
i leave to forgive me

■

turning

turning into my own
turning on in
to my own self
at last
turning out of the
white cage, turning out of the
lady cage
turning at last
on a stem like a black fruit
in my own season
at last

■

my poem

a love person
from love people
out of the afrikan sun
under the sign of cancer.
whoever see my
midnight smile
seeing star apple and
mango from home.
whoever take me for
a negative thing,
his death be on him
like a skin
and his skin
be his heart's revenge.

■

lucy one-eye
she got her mama's ways.
big round roller
can't cook
can't clean
if that's what you want
you got it world.

lucy one-eye
she see the world sideways.
word foolish
she say what she don't want
to say, she don't say
what she want to.

lucy one-eye
she won't walk away
from it.
she'll keep on trying
with her crooked look
and her wrinkled ways,
the darling girl.

■

if mama
could see
she would see
lucy sprawling
limbs of lucy
decorating the
backs of chairs
lucy hair
holding the mirrors up
that reflect odd
aspects of lucy.

if mama
could hear
she would hear
lucysong rolled in the
corners like lint
exotic webs of lucysighs
long lucy spiders explaining
to obscure gods.

if mama
could talk
she would talk
good girl
good girl
good girl
clean up your room.

■

i was born in a hotel,
a maskmaker.
my bones were knit by
a perilous knife.
my skin turned around
at midnight and
i entered the earth in
a woman jar.
i learned the world all
wormside up
and this is my yes
my strong fingers;
i was born in a bed of
good lessons
and it has made me
wise.

■

light
on my mother's tongue
breaks through her soft
extravagant hip
into life.
lucille
she calls the light,
which was the name
of the grandmother
who waited by the crossroads
in virginia
and shot the whiteman off his horse,
killing the killer of sons.
light breaks from her life
to her lives . . .

mine already is
an afrikan name.

■

cutting greens

curling them around
i hold their bodies in obscene embrace
thinking of everything but kinship.
collards and kale
strain against each strange other
away from my kissmaking hand and
the iron bedpot.
the pot is black,
the cutting board is black,
my hand,
and just for a minute
the greens roll black under the knife,
and the kitchen twists dark on its spine
and i taste in my natural appetite
the bond of live things everywhere.

■

i went to the valley
but i didn't go to stay

i stand on my father's ground
not breaking.
it holds me up
like a hand my father pushes.
virginia.
i am in virginia,
the magic word
rocked in my father's box
like heaven,
the magic line in my hand. but
where is the afrika in this?

except, the grass is green,
is greener he would say.
and the sky opens a better blue
and in the historical museum
where the slaves
are still hidden away like knives
i find a paper with a name i know.
his name.
their name.
sayles.
the name he loved.

i stand on my father's ground
not breaking.
there is an afrikan in this
and whose ever name it has been,
the blood is mine.

my soul got happy
and i stayed all day.

■

at last we killed the roaches.
mama and me. she sprayed,
i swept the ceiling and they fell
dying onto our shoulders, in our hair
covering us with red. the tribe was broken,
the cooking pots were ours again
and we were glad, such cleanliness was grace
when i was twelve. only for a few nights,
and then not much, my dreams were blood
my hands were blades and it was murder murder
all over the place.

■

in the evenings

i go through my rooms
like a witch watchman
mad as my mother was for
rattling knobs and
tapping glass. ah, lady,
i can see you now,
our personal nurse,
placing the iron
wrapped in rags
near our cold toes.
you are thawed places and
safe walls to me as i walk
the same sentry,
ironing the winters warm and
shaking locks in the night
like a ghost.

■

breaklight

light keeps on breaking.
i keep knowing
the language of other nations.
i keep hearing
tree talk
water words
and i keep knowing what they mean.
and light just keeps on breaking.
last night
the fears of my mother came
knocking and when i
opened the door
they tried to explain themselves
and i understood
everything they said.

■

some dreams hang in the air
like smoke. some dreams
get all in your clothes and
be wearing them more than you do and
you be half the time trying to
hold them and half the time
trying to wave them away.
their smell be all over you and
they get to your eyes and
you cry. the fire be gone
and the wood but some dreams
hang in the air like smoke
touching everything.

■

the thirty eighth year
of my life,
plain as bread
round as a cake
an ordinary woman.

an ordinary woman.

i had expected to be
smaller than this,
more beautiful,
wiser in afrikan ways,
more confident,
i had expected
more than this.

i will be forty soon.
my mother once was forty.

my mother died at forty four,
a woman of sad countenance
leaving behind a girl
awkward as a stork.
my mother was thick,
her hair was a jungle and
she was very wise
and beautiful
and sad.

i have dreamed dreams
for you mama
more than once.
i have wrapped me
in your skin
and made you live again

more than once.
i have taken the bones you hardened
and built daughters
and they blossom and promise fruit
like afrikan trees.
i am a woman now.
an ordinary woman.

in the thirty eighth
year of my life,
surrounded by life,
a perfect picture of
blackness blessed,
i had not expected this
loneliness.

if it is western,
if it is the final
europe in my mind,
if in the middle of my life
i am turning the final turn
into the shining dark
let me come to it whole
and holy
not afraid
not lonely
out of my mother's life
into my own.
into my own.

i had expected more than this.
i had not expected to be
an ordinary woman.

■

Anniversary

5/10/74

sixteen years
by the white of my hair
by my wide bones
by the life that ran out of me
into life,
sixteen years
and the girl is gone
with her two good eyes;
she was always hoping something,
she was afraid of everything.
little is left of her who hid
behind bread and babies
only something thin and
bright as a flame,
it has no language it can speak
without burning
it has no other house to run to
it loves you loves you loves you.

■

November 1, 1975

My mother is white bones
in a weed field
on her birthday.
She who would be sixty
has been sixteen years
absent at celebrations.
For sixteen years of minutes
she has been what is missing.
This is just to note
the arrogance of days
continuing to happen
as if she were here.

■

"We Do Not Know Very Much About Lucille's Inner Life"

from the light of her inner life
a company of citizens
watches lucille as she trembles
through the world.
she is a tired woman though
well meaning, they say.
when will she learn to listen to us?
lucille things are not what they seem.
all all is wonder and
astonishment.

■

lucy and her girls

lucy is the ocean
extended by
her girls
are the river
fed by
lucy
is the sun
reflected through
her girls
are the moon
lighted by
lucy
is the history of
her girls
are the place where
lucy
was going

■

i was born with twelve fingers
like my mother and my daughter.
each of us
born wearing strange black gloves
extra baby fingers hanging over the sides of our cribs and
dipping into the milk.
somebody was afraid we would learn to cast spells
and our wonders were cut off
but they didn't understand
the powerful memories of ghosts.   now
we take what we want
with invisible fingers
and we connect
my dead mother   my live daughter   and me
through our terrible shadowy hands.

■

what the mirror said

listen,
you a wonder.
you a city
of a woman.
you got a geography
of your own.
listen,
somebody need a map
to understand you.
somebody need directions
to move around you.
listen,
woman,
you not a noplace
anonymous
girl;
mister with his hands on you
he got his hands on
some
damn
body!

■

there is a girl inside.
she is randy as a wolf.
she will not walk away
and leave these bones
to an old woman.

she is a green tree
in a forest of kindling.
she is a green girl
in a used poet.

she has waited
patient as a nun
for the second coming,
when she can break through gray hairs
into blossom

and her lovers will harvest
honey and thyme
and the woods will be wild
with the damn wonder of it.

■

to merle

say skinny manysided tall on the ball
brown downtown woman
last time i saw you was on the corner of
pyramid and sphinx.
ten thousand years have interrupted our conversation
but I have kept most of my words
till you came back.
what i'm trying to say is
i recognize your language and
let me call you sister, sister,
i been waiting for you.

■

august the 12th
for sam

we are two scars on a dead woman's belly
brother, cut from the same knife
you and me. today is your birthday.
where are you? my hair
is crying for her brother.
myself with a mustache
empties the mirror on our mother's table
and all the phones in august wait.
today is your birthday, call us.
tell us where you are,
tell us why you are silent now.

■

speaking of loss

i began with everything;
parents, two extra fingers
a brother to ruin. i was
a rich girl with no money
in a red dress. how did i come
to sit in this house
wearing a name i never heard
until i was a woman? someone has stolen
my parents and hidden my brother.
my extra fingers are cut away.
i am left with plain hands and
nothing to give you but poems.

■

february 13, 1980

twenty-one years of my life you have been
the lost color in my eye. my secret blindness,
all my seeings turned gray with your going.
mother, i have worn your name like a shield.
it has torn but protected me all these years,
now even your absence comes of age.
i put on a dress called woman for this day
but i am not grown away from you
whatever i say.

■

new year

lucy
by sam
out of thelma
limps down a ramp
toward the rest of her life.
with too many candles
in her hair
she is a princess of
burning buildings
leaving the year that
tried to consume her.
her hands are bright
as they witch for water
and even her tears cry
fire   fire
but she opens herself
to the risk of flame and
walks toward an ocean
of days.

■

sonora desert poem
for lois and richard shelton

1.

the ones who live in the desert,
if you knew them
you would understand everything.
they see it all and
never judge any
just drink the water when
they get the chance.
if i could grow arms on my scars
like them,
if i could learn
the patience they know
i wouldn't apologize for my thorns either
just stand in the desert
and witness.

2. directions for watching the sun set in the desert

come to the landscape that was hidden under the sea.
look in the opposite direction.
reach for the mountain.
the mountain will ignore your hand.
the sun will fall on your back.
the landscape will fade away.
you will think you're alone until a flash
of green incredible light.

3. directions for leaving the desert

push the bones back
under your skin.
finish the water.
they will notice your thorns and
ask you to testify.
turn toward the shade.
smile.
say nothing at all.

■

my friends

no they will not understand
when i throw off my legs and my arms
at your hesitant yes.
when i throw them off and slide
like a marvelous snake toward your bed
your box   whatever you will keep me in
no   they will not understand what can be
so valuable beyond paper dollars diamonds
what is to me worth all appendages.
they will never understand   never approve
of me loving at last where i would
throw it all off to be,
with you   in your small room   limbless
but whole.

■

i once knew a man

i once knew a man who had wild horses killed.
when he told about it
the words came galloping out of his mouth
and shook themselves and headed off in
every damn direction. his tongue
was wild and wide and spinning when he talked
and the people he looked at closed their eyes
and tore the skins off their backs as they walked away
and stopped eating meat.
there was no holding him once he got started;
he had had wild horses killed one time and
they rode him to his grave.

■

the mystery that surely is present
as the underside of a leaf
turning to stare at you quietly
from your hand,
that is the mystery you have not
looked for, and it turns
with a silent shattering of your life
for who knows ever after
the proper position of things
or what is waiting to turn from us
even now?

■

the astrologer predicts at mary's birth

this one lie down on grass.
this one old men will follow
calling mother   mother.
she womb will blossom then die.
this one she hide from evening.
at a certain time when she hear something
it will burn her ear.
at a certain place when she see something
it will break her eye.

■

a song of mary

somewhere it being yesterday.
i a maiden in my mother's house.
the animals silent outside.
is morning.
princes sitting on thrones in the east
studying the incomprehensible heavens.
joseph carving a table somewhere
in another place.
i watching my mother.
i smiling an ordinary smile.

■

island mary

after the all been done and i
one old creature carried on
another creature's back, i wonder
could i have fought these thing?
surrounded by no son of mine save
old men calling mother like in the tale
the astrologer tell, i wonder
could i have walk away when voices
singing in my sleep? i one old woman.
always i seem to worrying now for
another young girl asleep
in the plain evening.
what song around her ear?
what star still choosing?

■

mary   mary astonished by God
on a straw bed circled by beasts
and an old husband. mary marinka
holy woman split by sanctified seed
into mother and mother for ever and ever
we pray for you sister woman shook by the
awe full affection of the saints.

■

the light that came to lucille clifton
came in a shift of knowing
when even her fondest sureties
faded away. it was the summer
she understood that she had not understood
and was not mistress even
of her own off eye. then
the man escaped throwing away his tie and
the children grew legs and started walking and
she could see the peril of an
unexamined life.
she closed her eyes, afraid to look for her
authenticity
but the light insists on itself in the world;
a voice from the nondead past started talking,
she closed her ears and it spelled out in her hand
"you might as well answer the door, my child,
 the truth is furiously knocking."

■

testament

in the beginning
was the word.

the year of our lord,
amen. i
lucille clifton
hereby testify
that in that room
there was a light
and in that light
there was a voice
and in that voice
there was a sigh
and in that sigh
there was a world.
a world a sigh a voice a light and
i
alone
in a room.

∎

mother, i am mad.
we should have guessed
a twelve-fingered flower
might break. my knowing
flutters to the ground.

mother i have managed to unlearn
my lessons. i am left
in otherness. mother

someone calling itself Light
has opened my inside.
i am flooded with brilliance
mother,

someone of it is answering to
your name.

■

to joan

joan
did you never hear
in the soft rushes of france
merely the whisper of french grass
rubbing against leathern
sounding now like a windsong
now like a man?
did you never wonder
oh fantastical joan,
did you never cry in the sun's face
unreal   unreal? did you never run
villageward
hands pushed out toward your apron?
and just as you knew that your mystery
was broken for all time
did they not fall then
soft as always
into your ear
calling themselves michael
among beloved others?
and you
sister   sister
did you not then sigh
my voices   my voices   of course?

■

in populated air
our ancestors continue.
i have seen them.
i have heard
their shimmering voices
singing.

■

there

there in the homelands
they are arresting children.
they are beating children
and shooting children.
                    in jo'burg
a woman sits on her veranda.
watching her child.
her child is playing on their lawn.
her man comes home from
arresting children. she smiles.
she offers him a drink.
each morning i practice for
getting that woman.
when her sister calls me sister
i remind myself
she is there.

■

this belief
in the magic of whiteness,
that it is the smooth
pebble in your hand,
that it is the godmother's
best gift,
that it explains,
allows,
assures,
entitles,
that it can sprout singular blossoms
like jack's bean
and singular verandas from which
to watch them rise,
it is a spell
winding round on itself,
grimms' awful fable,
and it turns into capetown and johannesburg
as surely as the beanstalk leads
to the giant's actual country
where jack lies broken at the
meadow's edge
and the land is in ruins,
no magic, no anything.

■

why some people be mad at me sometimes

they ask me to remember
but they want me to remember
their memories
and i keep on remembering
mine.

■

sorrow song

for the eyes of the children,
the last to melt,
the last to vaporize,
for the lingering
eyes of the children, staring,
the eyes of the children of
buchenwald,
of viet nam and johannesburg,
for the eyes of the children
of nagasaki,
for the eyes of the children
of middle passage,
for cherokee eyes, ethiopian eyes,
russian eyes, american eyes,
for all that remains of the children,
their eyes,
staring at us,   amazed to see
the extraordinary evil in
ordinary men.

■

them bones
them bones will
rise again
them bones
them bones will
walk again
them bones
them bones will
talk again
now hear
the word of The Lord
                    —Traditional

atlantic is a sea of bones,
my bones,
my elegant afrikans
connecting whydah and new york,
a bridge of ivory.

seabed they call it.
in its arms my early mothers sleep.
some women leapt with babies in their arms.
some women wept and threw the babies in.

maternal armies pace the atlantic floor.
i call my name into the roar of surf
and something awful answers.

■

cruelty. don't talk to me about cruelty
or what I am capable of.

when i wanted the roaches dead i wanted them dead
and i killed them. i took a broom to their country

and smashed and sliced without warning
without stopping and i smiled all the time i was doing it.

it was a holocaust of roaches, bodies,
parts of bodies, red all over the ground.

i didn't ask their names.
they had no names worth knowing.

now i watch myself whenever i enter a room.
i never know what i might do.

■

the lost women

i need to know their names
those women I would have walked with
jauntily the way men go in groups
swinging their arms, and the ones
those sweating women whom I would have joined
after a hard game to chew the fat
what would we have called each other laughing
joking into our beer? where are my gangs,
my teams, my mislaid sisters?
all the women who could have known me,
where in the world are their names?

■

my dream about the cows

and then i see the cattle of my own town,
rustled already,
prodded by pale cowboys with a foreign smell
into dark pens built to hold them forever,
and then i see a few of them
rib thin and weeping low over
sparse fields and milkless lives but
standing somehow standing,
and then i see how all despair is
thin and weak and personal and
then i see it's only
the dream about the cows.

■

my dream about the second coming

mary is an old woman without shoes.
she doesn't believe it.
not when her belly starts to bubble
and leave the print of a finger where
no man touches.
not when the snow in her hair melts away.
not when the stranger she used to wait for
appears dressed in lights at her
kitchen table.
she is an old woman and
doesn't believe it.

when Something drops onto her toes one night
she calls it a fox
but she feeds it.

■

the death of thelma sayles
2/13/59
age 44

i leave no tracks so my live loves
can't follow. at the river
most turn back, their souls shivering,
but my little girl stands alone on the bank
and watches. i pull my heart out of my pocket
and throw it. i smile as she catches all
she'll ever catch and heads for home
and her children. mothering
has made it strong, i whisper in her ear
along the leaves.

■

the message of thelma sayles

baby, my only husband turned away.
for twenty years my door was open.
nobody ever came.

the first fit broke my bed.
i woke from ecstasy to ask
what blood is this? am i the bride of Christ?
my bitten tongue was swollen for three days.

i thrashed and rolled from fit to death.
you are my only daughter.

when you lie awake in the evenings
counting your birthdays
turn the blood that clots your tongue
into poems. poems.

■

the death of joanne c.
11/30/82
aged 21

i am the battleground that
shrieks like a girl.
to myself i call myself
gettysburg. laughing,
twisting the i.v.,
laughing or crying, i can't tell
which anymore,
i host the furious battling of
a suicidal body and
a murderous cure.

■

enter my mother
wearing a peaked hat.
her cape billows,
her broom sweeps the nurses away,
she is flying, the witch of the ward, my mother
pulls me up by the scruff of the spine
incanting   Live   Live   Live!

■

leukemia as white rabbit

running always running murmuring
she will be furious   she will be
furious, following a great
cabbage of a watch that tells only
terminal time, down deep into a
rabbit hole of diagnosticians shouting
off with her hair   off with her skin and
i am   i am   i am   furious.

■

chemotherapy

my hair is pain.
my mouth is a cave of cries.
my room is filled with white coats
shaped like God.
they are moving their fingers along
their stethoscopes.
they are testing their chemical faith.
chemicals   chemicals   oh mother mary
where is your living child?

■

the message of jo

my body is a war
nobody is winning.
my birthdays are tired.
my blood is a white flag,
waving.
surrender,
my darling mother,
death is life.

■

the death of fred clifton
11/10/84
age 49

i seemed to be drawn
to the center of myself
leaving the edges of me
in the hands of my wife
and i saw with the most amazing
clarity
so that i had not eyes but
sight,
and, rising and turning
through my skin,
there was all around not the
shapes of things
but oh, at last, the things
themselves.

■

"i'm going back to my true identity"
fjc 11/84

i was ready to return
to my rightful name.
i saw it hovering near
in blazoned script
and, passing through fire,
i claimed it. here
is a box of stars
for my living wife.
tell her to scatter them
pronouncing no name.
tell her there is no deathless name
a body can pronounce.

■

in white america

1   i come to read them poems

i come to read them poems,
a fancy trick i do
like juggling with balls of light.
i stand, a dark spinner,
in the grange hall,
in the library, in the
smaller conference room,
and toss and catch as if by magic,
my eyes bright, my mouth smiling,
my singed hands burning.

2   the history

1800's in this town
fourteen longhouses were destroyed
by not these people here.
not these people
burned the crops and chopped down
all the peach trees.
not these people. these people
preserve peaches, even now.

3   the tour

"this was a female school.
my mother's mother graduated
second in her class.
they were taught embroidery,
and chenille and filigree,
ladies' learning. yes,

we have a liberal history here."
smiling she pats my darky hand.

4   *the hall*

in this hall
dark women
scrubbed the aisles
between the pews
on their knees.
they could not rise
to worship.
in this hall
dark women
my sisters and mothers

though i speak with the tongues
of men and of angels and
have not charity . . .

in this hall
dark women,
my sisters and mothers,
i stand
and let the church say
let the church say
let the church say
AMEN.

5   *the reading*

i look into none of my faces
and do the best i can.
the human hair between us
stretches but does not break.

i slide myself along it and
love them, love them all.

6   *it is late*

it is late
in white america.
i stand
in the light of the
7-11
looking out toward
the church
and for a moment only
i feel the reverberation
of myself
in white america
a black cat
in the belfry
hanging
and
ringing.

■

shapeshifter poems

1

the legend is whispered
in the women's tent
how the moon when she rises
full
follows some men into themselves
and changes them there
the season is short
but dreadful   shapeshifters
they wear strange hands
they walk through the houses
at night   their daughters
do not know them

2

who is there to protect her
from the hands of the father
not the windows which see and
say nothing   not the moon
that awful eye   not the woman
she will become with her
scarred tongue   who   who   who   the owl
laments into the evening   who
will protect her   this   prettylittlegirl

3

if the little girl lies
still enough
shut enough

hard enough
shapeshifter may not
walk tonight
the full moon may not
find him here
the hair on him
bristling
rising
up

4

the poem at the end of the world
is the poem the little girl breathes
into her pillow   the one
she cannot tell   the one
there is no one to hear   this poem
is a political poem   is a war poem   is a
universal poem but is not about
these things   this poem
is about one human heart   this poem
is the poem at the end of the world

■

i am accused of tending to the past
as if i made it,
as if i sculpted it
with my own hands. i did not.
this past was waiting for me
when i came,
a monstrous unnamed baby,
and i with my mother's itch
took it to breast
and named it
History.
she is more human now,
learning language everyday,
remembering faces, names and dates.
when she is strong enough to travel
on her own, beware, she will.

■

note to myself

it's a black thing you wouldn't understand
                                        (t-shirt)

amira baraka—*i refuse to be judged by white men.*

or defined. and i see
that even the best believe
they have that right,
believe that
what they say i mean
is what i mean
as if words only matter in the world they know,
as if when i choose words
i must choose those
that they can live with
even if something inside me
cannot live,
as if my story is
so trivial
we can forget together,
as if i am not scarred,
as if my family enemy
does not look like them,
as if i have not reached
across our history to touch,
to soothe on more than one
occasion
and will again,
although the merely human
is denied me still
and i am now no longer beast
but saint.

■

poem beginning in no and ending in yes

for hector peterson, age 13
first child killed in soweto riot, 1976

no
light there was no light at first around the head
of the young boy   only the slim stirring of soweto
only the shadow of voices   students and soldiers
practicing their lessons   and one and one cannot be even
two in afrikaans   then before the final hush
in the schoolyard in soweto   there was the burning of his name
into the most amazing science   the most ancient prophesy
let there be light and there was light around the young
boy hector peterson dead in soweto and still among us
yes

■

slave cabin, sotterly plantation, maryland, 1989

in this little room
note carefully

aunt nanny's bench

three words that label
things
aunt
is my parent's sister
nanny
my grandmother
bench
the board at which
i stare
the soft curved polished
wood
that held her bottom
after the long days
without end
without beginning
when she   aunt nanny   sat
feet dead against the dirty floor
humming for herself   humming
her own sweet human name

■

whose side are you on?

the side of the busstop woman
trying to drag her bag
up the front steps before the doors
clang shut   i am on her side
i give her exact change
and him the old man hanging by
one strap his work hand folded shut
as the bus doors i am on his side
when he needs to leave
i ring the bell   i am on their side
riding the late bus into the same
someplace   i am on the dark side always
the side of my daughters
the side of my tired sons

■

shooting star

who would i expect
to understand
what it be like
what it be like
living under a star
that hates you. you
spend a half life
looking for your own
particular heaven,
expecting to be found
one day on a sidewalk
in a bad neighborhood,
face toward the sky,
hoping some body saw
a blaze of light perhaps
a shooting star
some thing to make it mean
some thing.   yo,
that brilliance there,
is it you, huey?
is it huey?
is it you?

> *for huey p. newton*
> *r.i.p.*

■

this is for the mice that live
behind the baseboard,
she whispered, her fingers
thick with cheese. what i do
is call them, copying their own
voices; please please please
sweet please. i promise
them nothing. they come
bringing nothing and we sit
together, nuzzling each other's
hungry hands. everything i want
i have to ask for, she sighed.

■

man and wife

she blames him, at the last, for
backing away from his bones
and his woman, from the life
he promised her was worth
cold sheets. she blames him
for being unable to see
the tears in her eyes, the birds
hovered by the window, for love being
not enough, for leaving.

he blames her, at the last, for
holding him back with her eyes
beyond when the pain was more
than he was prepared to bear,
for the tears he could neither
end nor ignore, for believing
that love could be enough,
for the birds, for the life
so difficult to leave.

■

poem in praise of menstruation

if there is a river
more beautiful than this
bright as the blood
red edge of the moon   if

there is a river
more faithful than this
returning each month
to the same delta   if there

is a river
braver than this
coming and coming in a surge
of passion, of pain   if there is

a river
more ancient than this
daughter of eve
mother of cain and of abel   if there is in

the universe such a river   if
there is some where water
more powerful than this wild
water
pray that it flows also
through animals
beautiful and faithful and ancient
and female and brave

■

the killing of the trees

the third went down
with a sound almost like flaking,
a soft swish as the left leaves
fluttered themselves and died.
three of them, four, then five
stiffening in the snow
as if this hill were Wounded Knee
as if the slim feathered branches
were bonnets of war
as if the pale man seated
high in the bulldozer nest
his blonde mustache ice-matted
was Pahuska come again but stronger now,
his long hair wild and unrelenting.

remember the photograph,
the old warrior, his stiffened arm
raised as if in blessing,
his frozen eyes open,
his bark skin brown and not so much
wrinkled as circled with age,
and the snow everywhere still falling,
covering his one good leg.
remember his name was Spotted Tail
or Hump or Red Cloud or Geronimo
or none of these or all of these.
he was a chief. he was a tree
falling the way a chief falls,
straight, eyes open, arms reaching
for his mother ground.

so i have come to live
among the men who kill the trees,
a subdivision, new,

in southern Maryland.
I have brought my witness eye with me
and my two wild hands,
the left one sister to the fists
pushing the bulldozer against the old oak,
the angry right, brown and hard and spotted
as bark. we come in peace,
but this morning
ponies circle what is left of life
and whales and continents and children and ozone
and trees huddle in a camp weeping
outside my window and i can see it all
with that one good eye.

∎

pahuska=long hair, lakota name for custer

wild blessings

licked in the palm of my hand
by an uninvited woman. so i have held
in that hand the hand of a man who
emptied into his daughter, the hand
of a girl who threw herself
from a tenement window, the trembling
junkie hand of a priest, of a boy who
shattered across viet nam
someone resembling his mother,
and more. and more.
do not ask me to thank the tongue
that circled my fingers
or pride myself on the attentions
of the holy lost.
i am grateful for many blessings
but the gift of understanding,
the wild one, maybe not.

■

somewhere
some woman
just like me
tests the lock on the window
in the children's room,
lays out tomorrow's school clothes,
sets the table for breakfast early,
finds a pen between the cushions
on the couch
sits down and writes the words
Good Times.
i think of her as i begin to teach
the lives of the poets,
about her space at the table
and my own inexplicable life.

■

1

when i stand around among poets
i am embarrassed mostly,
their long white heads,
the great bulge in their pants,

their certainties.

i don't know how to do
what i do in the way
that i do it. it happens
despite me and i pretend

to deserve it.

but i don't know how to do it.
only sometimes when
something is singing
i listen and so far

i hear.

2

when i stand around
among poets, sometimes
i hear a single music
in us, one note
dancing us through the
singular moving world.

■

water sign woman

the woman who feels everything
sits in her new house
waiting for someone to come
who knows how to carry water
without spilling, who knows
why the desert is sprinkled
with salt, why tomorrow
is such a long and ominous word.

they say to the feel things woman
that little she dreams is possible,
that there is only so much
joy to go around, only so much
water. there are no questions
for this, no arguments. she has

to forget to remember the edge
of the sea, they say, to forget
how to swim to the edge, she has
to forget how to feel. the woman
who feels everything sits in her
new house retaining the secret
the desert knew when it walked
up from the ocean, the desert,

so beautiful in her eyes;
water will come again
if you can wait for it.
she feels what the desert feels.
she waits.

■

photograph

my grandsons
spinning in their joy

universe
keep them turning   turning
black blurs against the window
of the world
for they are beautiful
and there is trouble coming
round and round and round

■

december 7, 1989

this morning your grandmother
sits in the shadow of
Pearl drinking her coffee.
a sneak attack would find me
where my mother sat that day,
flush against her kitchen table,
her big breasts leaning into
the sugar spill. and it is sweet
to be here in the space between
one horror and another
thinking that history
happens all the time
but is remembered backward
in labels not paragraphs.
and so i claim this day
and offer it
this paragraph i own
to you, peyo, dakotah,
for when you need some
memory, some honey thing
to taste, and call the past.

■

to my friend, jerina

listen,
when i found there was no safety
in my father's house
i knew there was none anywhere.
you are right about this,
how i nurtured my work
not my self, how i left the girl
wallowing in her own shame
and took on the flesh of my mother.
but listen,
the girl is rising in me,
not willing to be left to
the silent fingers in the dark,
and you are right,
she is asking for more than
most men are able to give,
but she means to have what she
has earned,
sweet sighs, safe houses,
hands she can trust.

■

poem to my uterus

you   uterus
you have been patient
as a sock
while i have slippered into you
my dead and living children
now
they want to cut you out
stocking i will not need
where i am going
where am i going
old girl
without you
uterus
my bloody print
my estrogen kitchen
my black bag of desire
where can i go
barefoot
without you
where can you go
without me

■

to my last period

well girl, goodbye,
after thirty-eight years.
thirty-eight years and you
never arrived
splendid in your red dress
without trouble for me
somewhere, somehow

now it is done
and i feel just like
the grandmothers who,
after the hussy has gone,
sit holding her photograph
and sighing, *wasn't she
beautiful? wasn't she beautiful?*

■

the mother's story

a line of women i don't know,
she said,
came in and whispered over you
each one fierce word,
she said, each word
more powerful than one before.
and i thought what is this to bring
to one black girl from buffalo
until the last one came and smiled,
she said,
and filled your ear with light
and that, she said, has been the one,
the last one, that last one.

■

as he was dying
a canticle of birds
hovered
watching through the glass
as if to catch
that final breath
and sing it   where?
he died.
there was a shattering of wing
that sounded   then did not sound,
and we stood in this silence
blackly   some would say,
while through the windows,
as perhaps at other times,
the birds, if they had stayed,
could see us,
and i do not mean white here,
but as we are,
transparent women and transparent men.

■

blessing the boats

(at St. Mary's)

may the tide
that is entering even now
the lip of our understanding
carry you out
beyond the face of fear
may you kiss
the wind then turn from it
certain that it will
love your back   may you
open your eyes to water
water waving forever
and may you in your innocence
sail through this to that

■

LIGHT

ray
stream
gleam
beam
sun
glow
flicker
shine
lucid
spark
scintilla
flash
blaze
flame
fire
serene
luciferous
lightning bolt
luster
shimmer
glisten
gloss
brightness
brilliance
splendor
sheen
dazzle
sparkle
luminous
reflection
kindle
illuminate
brighten
glorious

radiate
radiant
splendid
clarify
clear

ROGET'S THESAURUS

■

june 20

i will be born in one week
to a frowned forehead of a woman
and a man whose fingers will itch
to enter me. she will crochet
a dress for me of silver
and he will carry me in it.
they will do for each other
all that they can
but it will not be enough.
none of us know that we will not
smile again for years,
that she will not live long.
in one week i will emerge face first
into their temporary joy.

■

daughters

woman who shines at the head
of my grandmother's bed,
brilliant woman, i like to think
you whispered into her ear
instructions. i like to think
you are the oddness in us,
you are the arrow
that pierced our plain skin
and made us fancy women;
my wild witch gran, my magic mama,
and even these gaudy girls.
i like to think you gave us
extraordinary power and to
protect us, you became the name
we were cautioned to forget.
it is enough,
you must have murmured,
to remember that i was
and that you are. woman, i am
lucille, which stands for light,
daughter of thelma, daughter
of georgia, daughter of
dazzling you.

■

sam

if he could have kept
the sky in his dark hand
he would have pulled it down
and held it.
it would have called him lord
as did the skinny women
in virginia. if he
could have gone to school
he would have learned to write
his story and not live it.
if he could have done better
he would have. oh stars
and stripes forever,
what did you do to my father?

■

thel

was my first landscape,
red brown as the clay
of her georgia.
sweet attic of a woman,
repository of old songs.
there was such music in her;
she would sit, shy as a wren
humming alone and lonely
amid broken promises,
amid the sweet broken bodies
of birds.

■

11/10 again

some say the radiance around the body
can be seen by eyes latticed against
all light but the particular. they say
you can notice something rise
from the houseboat of the body
wearing the body's face,
and that you can feel the presence
of a possible otherwhere.
not mystical, they say, but human,
human to lift away from the arms that
try to hold you (as you did then)
and, brilliance magnified,
circle beyond the ironwork
encasing your human heart.

■

she lived

after he died
what really happened is
she watched the days
bundle into thousands,
watched every act become
the history of others,
every bed more
narrow,
but even as the eyes of lovers
strained toward the milky young
she walked away
from the hole in the ground
deciding to live.   and she lived.

■

won't you celebrate with me
what i have shaped into
a kind of life? i had no model.
born in babylon
both nonwhite and woman
what did i see to be except myself?
i made it up
here on this bridge between
starshine and clay,
my one hand holding tight
my other hand; come celebrate
with me that everyday
something has tried to kill me
and has failed.

■

it was a dream

in which my greater self
rose up before me
accusing me of my life
with her extra finger
whirling in a gyre of rage
at what my days had come to.
what,
i pleaded with her, could i do,
oh what could i have done?
and she twisted her wild hair
and sparked her wild eyes
and screamed as long as
i could hear her
This.   This.   This.

■

each morning i pull myself
out of despair

from a night of coals and a tongue
blistered with smiling

the step past the mother bed
is a high step

the walk through the widow's door
is a long walk

and who are these voices calling
from every mirrored thing

say it coward say it

■

here yet be dragons

so many languages have fallen
off of the edge of the world
into the dragon's mouth. some

where there be monsters whose teeth
are sharp and sparkle with lost

people. lost poems. who
among us can imagine ourselves
unimagined? who

among us can speak with so fragile
tongue and remain proud?

■

the earth is a living thing

is a black shambling bear
ruffling its wild back and tossing
mountains into the sea

is a black hawk circling
the burying ground circling the bones
picked clean and discarded

is a fish black blind in the belly of water
is a diamond blind in the black belly of coal

is a black and living thing
is a favorite child
of the universe
feel her rolling her hand
in its kinky hair
feel her brushing it clean

■

move

On May 13, 1985 Wilson Goode, Philadelphia's first Black mayor, authorized the bombing of 6221 Osage Avenue after the complaints of neighbors, also Black, about the Afrocentric back-to-nature group headquartered there and calling itself Move. All the members of the group wore dreadlocks and had taken the surname Africa. In the bombing eleven people, including children, were killed and sixty-one homes in the neighborhood were destroyed.

they had begun to whisper
among themselves   hesitant
to be branded neighbor to the wild
haired women the naked children
reclaiming a continent
away

move

he hesitated
then turned his smoky finger
toward africa toward the house
he might have lived in might have
owned or saved had he not turned
away

move

the helicopter rose at the command
higher at first then hesitating
then turning toward the center
of its own town only a neighborhood
away

move

she cried as the child stood
hesitant in the last clear sky
he would ever see   the last
before the whirling blades the whirling smoke
and sharp debris carried all clarity
away

move

if you live in a mind
that would destroy itself
to comfort itself
if you would stand fire
rather than difference
do not hesitate
move
away

■

samson predicts from gaza
the philadelphia fire

for ramona africa, survivor

it will be your hair
ramona africa
they will come for you
they will bring fire
they will empty your eyes
of everything you love
your hair will writhe
and hiss on your shoulder
they will order you
to give it up   if you do
you will bring the temple down
if you do not   they will

■

if i should

to clark kent

enter the darkest room
in my house and speak
with my own voice, at last,
about its awful furniture,
pulling apart the covering
over the dusty bodies; the randy
father, the husband holding ice
in his hand like a blessing,
the mother bleeding into herself
and the small imploding girl,
i say if i should walk into
that web, who will come flying
after me, leaping tall buildings?
you?

■

further note to clark

do you know how hard this is for me?
do you know what you're asking?

what i can promise to be is water,
water plain and direct as Niagara.
unsparing of myself, unsparing of
the cliff i batter, but also unsparing
of you, tourist. the question for me is
how long can i cling to this edge?
the question for you is
what have you ever traveled toward
more than your own safety?

■

begin here

in the dark
where the girl is
sleeping
begin with a shadow
rising on the wall
no
begin with a spear
of salt like a tongue
no
begin with a swollen
horn   or finger
no
no   begin here
something in the girl
is wakening   some
thing in the girl
is falling
deeper and deeper
asleep

■

night vision

the girl fits her body in
to the space between the bed
and the wall. she is a stalk,
exhausted. she will do some
thing with this. she will
surround these bones with flesh.
she will cultivate night vision.
she will train her tongue
to lie still in her mouth and listen.
the girl slips into sleep.
her dream is red and raging.
she will remember
to build something human with it.

■

fury

for mama

remember this.
she is standing by
the furnace.
the coals
glisten like rubies.
her hand is crying.
her hand is clutching
a sheaf of papers.
poems.
she gives them up.
they burn
jewels into jewels.
her eyes are animals.
each hank of her hair
is a serpent's obedient
wife.
she will never recover.
remember. there is nothing
you will not bear
for this woman's sake.

■

cigarettes

my father burned us all. ash
fell from his hand onto our beds,
onto our tables and chairs.
ours was the roof the sirens
rushed to at night
mistaking the glow of his pain
for flame. nothing is burning here,
my father would laugh, ignoring
my charred pillow, ignoring his own
smoldering halls.

■

leda   1

there is nothing luminous
about this.
they took my children.
i live alone in the backside
of the village.
my mother moved
to another town. my father
follows me around the well,
his thick lips slavering,
and at night my dreams are full
of the cursing of me
fucking god fucking me.

■

leda 2

a note on visitations

sometimes another star chooses.
the ones coming in from the east
are dagger-fingered men,
princes of no known kingdom.
the animals are raised up in their stalls
battering the stable door.
sometimes it all goes badly;
the inn is strewn with feathers,
the old husband suspicious,
and the fur between her thighs
is the only shining thing.

■

leda 3

always pyrotechnics;
stars spinning into phalluses
of light, serpents promising
sweetness, their forked tongues
thick and erect, patriarchs of bird
exposing themselves in the air.
this skin is sick with loneliness.
You want what a man wants,
next time come as a man
or don't come.

■

brothers

*(being a conversation in eight poems between an aged
Lucifer and God, though only Lucifer is heard. The time is
long after.)*

1
invitation

come coil with me
here in creation's bed
among the twigs and ribbons
of the past. i have grown old
remembering this garden,
the hum of the great cats
moving into language, the sweet
fume of man's rib
as it rose up and began to walk.
it was all glory then,
the winged creatures leaping
like angels, the oceans claiming
their own. let us rest here a time
like two old brothers
who watched it happen and wondered
what it meant.

2
how great Thou art

listen, You are beyond
even Your own understanding.
that rib and rain and clay
in all its pride,
its unsteady dominion,
is not what You believed

You were,
but it is what You are;
in Your own image as some
lexicographer supposed.
the face, both he and she,
the odd ambition, the desire
to reach beyond the stars
is You. all You, all You
the loneliness, the perfect
imperfection.

3
as for myself

less snake than angel
less angel than man
how come i to this
serpent's understanding?
watching creation from
a hood of leaves
i have foreseen the evening
of the world.
as sure as she,
the breast of Yourself
separated out and made to bear,
as sure as her returning,
i too am blessed with
the one gift you cherish;
to feel the living move in me
and to be unafraid.

4
in my own defense

what could i choose
but to slide along beside them,
they whose only sin
was being their father's children?
as they stood with their backs
to the garden,
a new and terrible luster
burning their eyes,
only You could have called
their ineffable names,
only in their fever
could they have failed to hear.

5
the road led from delight

into delight. into the sharp
edge of seasons, into the sweet
puff of bread baking, the warm
vale of sheet and sweat after love,
the tinny newborn cry of calf
and cormorant and humankind.
and pain, of course,
always there was some bleeding,
but forbid me not
my meditation on the outer world
before the rest of it, before
the bruising of his heel, my head,
and so forth.

6
"the silence of God is God."
  —Carolyn Forché

tell me, tell us why
in the confusion of a mountain
of babies stacked like cordwood,
of limbs walking away from each other,
of tongues bitten through
by the language of assault,
tell me, tell us why
You neither raised Your hand
nor turned away, tell us why
You watched the excommunication of
that world and You said nothing.

7
still there is mercy, there is grace

how otherwise
could i have come to this
marble spinning in space
propelled by the great
thumb of the universe?
how otherwise
could the two roads
of this tongue
converge into a single
certitude?
how otherwise
could i, a sleek old
traveler,
curl one day safe and still
beside You
at Your feet, perhaps,
but, amen, Yours.

8
"...........is God."

so.
having no need to speak
You sent Your tongue
splintered into angels.
even i,
with my little piece of it
have said too much.
to ask You to explain
is to deny You.
before the word
You were.
You kiss my brother mouth.
the rest is silence.

■

hometown
1993

think of it; the landscape
potted as if by war, think of
the weeds, the boarded buildings,
the slivers of window abandoned
in the streets, and behind one
glass, my little brother, dying.
think of how he must have
bounded into our mothers arms,
held hard to our fathers swollen hand,
never looking back, glad to be gone
from the contempt, the terrible night
of buffalo.

■

ones like us

enter a blurry world,
fetish tight around our
smallest finger, mezuzah
gripped in our good child hand.
we feel for our luck
but everywhere is menace   menace
until we settle ourselves
against the bark of trees, against
the hide of fierce protection
and there, in the shadow,
words call us.   words call us
and we go.

for wayne karlin
5/28/93

■

telling our stories

the fox came every evening to my door
asking for nothing. my fear
trapped me inside, hoping to dismiss her
but she sat till morning, waiting.

at dawn we would, each of us,
rise from our haunches, look through the glass
then walk away.

did she gather her village around her
and sing of the hairless moon face,
the trembling snout, the ignorant eyes?

child, i tell you now it was not
the animal blood i was hiding from,
it was the poet in her, the poet and
the terrible stories she could tell.

■

the coming of fox

one evening i return
to a red fox
haunched by my door.

i am afraid
although she knows
no enemy comes here.

next night again
then next then next
she sits in her safe shadow

silent as my skin bleeds
into long bright flags
of fur.

■

dear fox

it is not my habit
to squat in the hungry desert
fingering stones, begging them
to heal, not me but the dry mornings
and bitter nights.
it is not your habit
to watch. none of this
is ours, sister fox.
tell yourself that anytime now
we will rise and walk away
from somebody else's life.
any time.

■

leaving fox

so many fuckless days and nights.
only the solitary fox
watching my window light
barks her compassion.
i move away from her eyes,
from the pitying brush
of her tail
to a new place and check
for signs. so far
i am the only animal.
i will keep the door unlocked
until something human comes.

■

a dream of foxes

in the dream of foxes
there is a field
and a procession of women
clean as good children
no hollow in the world
surrounded by dogs
no fur clumped bloody
on the ground
only a lovely line
of honest women stepping
without fear or guilt or shame
safe through the generous fields

■

amazons

when the rookery of women
warriors all
each cupping one hand around
her remaining breast

daughters of dahomey
their name fierce on the planet

when they came to ask
who knows what you might have
to sacrifice   poet   amazon
there is no choice

then when they each
with one nipple lifted
beckoned to me
five generations removed

i rose
and ran to the telephone
to hear
    cancer   early detection   no
    mastectomy   not yet

there was nothing to say
my sisters swooped in a circle dance
audre was with them and i
had already written this poem

■

lumpectomy eve

all night i dream of lips
that nursed and nursed
and the lonely nipple

lost in loss and the need
to feed that turns at last
on itself   that will kill

its body for its hunger's sake
all night i hear the whispering
the soft

> love calls you to this knife
> for love   for love

all night it is the one breast
comforting the other

■

1994

i was leaving my fifty-eighth year
when a thumb of ice
stamped itself hard near my heart

you have your own story
you know about the fear the tears
the scar of disbelief

you know that the saddest lies
are the ones we tell ourselves
you know how dangerous it is

to be born with breasts
you know how dangerous it is
to wear dark skin

i was leaving my fifty-eighth year
when i woke into the winter
of a cold and mortal body

thin icicles hanging off
the one mad nipple weeping

have we not been good children
did we not inherit the earth

but you must know all about this
from your own shivering life

■

hag riding

why
is what i ask myself
maybe it is the afrikan in me
still trying to get home
after all these years
but when i wake to the heat of the morning
galloping down the highway of my life
something hopeful rises in me
rises and runs me out into the road
and i lob my fierce thigh high
over the rump of the day and honey
i ride   i ride

■

rust

we don't like rust,
it reminds us that we are dying.
　　　　　　—Brett Singer

are you saying that iron understands
time is another name for God?

that the rain-licked pot is holy?
that the pan abandoned in the house

is holy? are you saying that they
are sanctified now, our girlhood skillets

tarnishing in the kitchen?
are you saying we only want to remember

the heft of our mothers' handles,
their ebony patience, their shine?

■

shadows

in the latter days
you will come to a place
called memphis
there you will wait for a while
by the river mississippi
until you can feel the shadow
of another memphis and another
river. nile

wake up girl.
you dreaming.

the sign may be water or fire
or it may be the black earth
or the black blood under the earth
or it may be the syllables themselves
coded to you from your southern kin.

wake up girl.
i swear you dreaming.

memphis.
capital of the old kingdom
of ancient egypt at the apex
of the river across from
the great pyramids.
nile. born in the mountains
of the moon.

wake up girl,
this don't connect.

wait there.
in the shadow of your room

you may see another dusky woman
weakened by too much loss.
she will be dreaming a small boat
through centuries of water
into the white new world.
she will be weaving garments
of neglect.

wake up girl.
this don't mean nothing.

meaning is the river
of voices. meaning
is the patience of the moon.
meaning is the thread
running forever in shadow.

girl girl wake up.
somebody calling you.

■

entering the south

i have put on my mother's coat.
it is warm and familiar
as old fur
and i can hear hushed voices
through it.   too many
animals have died
to make this.   the sleeves
coil down toward my hands
like rope.   i will wear it
because she loved it
but the blood from it pools
on my shoulders
heavy and dark and alive.

■

the mississippi river empties
into the gulf

and the gulf enters the sea and so forth,
none of them emptying anything,
all of them carrying yesterday
forever on their white tipped backs,
all of them dragging forward tomorrow.
it is the great circulation
of the earth's body, like the blood
of the gods, this river in which the past
is always flowing. every water
is the same water coming round.
everyday someone is standing on the edge
of this river, staring into time,
whispering mistakenly:
only here. only now.

■

old man river

everything elegant
but this water

tables set with crystal
at the tea shop

miss lady patting her lips
with linen

horses pure stock
negras pure stock

everything clear
but this big muddy

water

don't say nothin'
must know somethin'

■

auction street

for angela mcdonald

consider the drum.
consider auction street
and the beat
throbbing up through our shoes,
through the trolley
so that it rides as if propelled
by hundreds, by thousands
of fathers and mothers
led in a coffle
to the block.

consider the block,
topside smooth as skin
almost translucent like a drum
that has been beaten
for the last time
and waits now to be honored
for the music it has had to bear.
then consider brother moses,
who heard from the mountaintop:
take off your shoes,
the ground you walk is holy.

■

memphis

. . . at the river i stand,
guide my feet, hold my hand

i was raised
on the shore
of lake erie
e is for escape

there are more s'es
in mississippi
than my mother had
sons

this river never knew
the kingdom of dahomey

the first s
begins in slavery
and ends in y
on the bluffs

of memphis
why are you here
the river wonders
northern born

looking across from buffalo
you look into canada   toronto
is the name of the lights
burning at night

the bottom of memphis
drops into the nightmare
of a little girl's fear
in fifteen minutes

they could be here
i could be there
mississippi
not the river   the state

schwerner
and chaney
and goodman

medgar

schwerner
and chaney
and goodman
and medgar

my mother had one son
he died gently near lake erie

some rivers flow back
toward the beginning
i never learned to swim

will i float or drown
in this memphis
on the mississippi river

what is this southland
what has this to do with egypt
or dahomey
or with me

so many questions
northern born

■

what comes after this

water earth fire air
i can scarcely remember
gushing down through my mother
onto the family bed
but the dirt of eviction
is still there
and the burning bodies of men
i have tried to love

through the southern blinds
narrow memories enter the room
i had not counted on ice
nor clay nor the uncertain hiss
of an old flame   water earth fire
it is always unexpected and
i wonder what is coming
after this   whether it is air
or it is nothing

■

blake

saw them glittering in the trees,
their quills erect among the leaves,
angels everywhere. we need new words
for what this is, this hunger entering our
loneliness like birds, stunning our eyes into rays
of hope. we need the flutter that can save
us, something that will swirl across the face
of what we have become and bring us grace.
back north, i sit again in my own home
dreaming of blake, searching the branches
for just one poem.

■

evening and my dead once husband
rises up from the spirit board
through trembled air   i moan
the names of our wayward sons
and ask him to explain   why
i fuss like a fishwife   why
cancer and terrible loneliness
and the wars against our people
and the room glimmers as if washed
in tears and out of the mist a hand
becomes flesh and i watch
as its pointing fingers spell

it does not help to know

■

in the same week

for samuel sayles, jr., 1938–1993

after the third day
the fingers of your folded hands
must have melted together
into perpetual prayer.
it was hot and buffalo.
nothing innocent could stay.

in the same week
stafford folded his tongue
and was gone. nothing
innocent is safe.

the frailty of love
falls from the newspaper
onto our bedroom floor
and we walk past not noticing.
the end of something simple
is happening here,

something essential. brother,
we burned you into little shells
and stars. we hold them hard,
attend too late to each,
mourn every necessary bit.
the angels shake their heads.
too little and too late.

■

heaven

my brother is crouched at the edge
looking down.
he has gathered a circle of cloudy
friends around him
and they are watching the world.

i can feel them there, i always could.
i used to try to explain to him
the afterlife,
and he would laugh. he is laughing now,

pointing toward me. "she was my sister,"
i feel him say,
"even when she was right, she was wrong."

■

lorena

it lay in my palm soft and trembled
as a new bird and i thought about
authority and how it always insisted
on itself, how it was master
of the man, how it measured him, never
was ignored or denied and how it promised
there would be sweetness if it was obeyed
just like the saints do, like the angels,
and i opened the window and held out my
uncupped hand. i swear to god,
i thought it could fly

■

in the meantime

Poem ending with a line from The Mahabharata,
quoted at the time of the first atomic blast.

the Lord of loaves and fishes
frowns as the children of
Haiti Somalia Bosnia Rwanda Everyhere
float onto the boats of their bellies
and die   in the meantime
someone who is not hungry sits to dine

we could have become
fishers of men
we could have been
a balm
a light
we have become
not what we were

in the mean time
that split apart with the atom
all roads began to lead
to these tables
these hungry children
this time
and

I am become Death   the destroyer of worlds.

■

the times

it is hard to remain human on a day
when birds perch weeping
in the trees and the squirrel eyes
do not look away but the dog ones do
in pity.
another child has killed a child
and i catch myself relieved that they are
white and i might understand except
that i am tired of understanding.
if this
alphabet could speak its own tongue
it would be all symbol surely;
the cat would hunch across the long table
and that would mean time is catching up,
and the spindle fish would run to ground
and that would mean the end is coming
and the grains of dust would gather themselves
along the streets and spell out:

these too are your children   this too is your child

■

dialysis

after the cancer, the kidneys
refused to continue.
they closed their thousand eyes.

blood fountains from the blind man's
arm and decorates the tile today.
somebody mops it up.

the woman who is over ninety
cries for her mother.   if our dead
were here they would save us.

we are not supposed to hate
the dialysis unit.   we are not
supposed to hate the universe.

this is not supposed to happen to me.
after the cancer the body refused
to lose any more.   even the poisons
were claimed and kept

until they threatened to destroy
the heart they loved.   in my dream
a house is burning.

something crawls out of the fire
cleansed and purified.
in my dream i call it light.

after the cancer i was so grateful
to be alive.   i am alive and furious.
Blessed be even this?

■

libation

north carolina, 1999

i offer to this ground,
this gin.
i imagine an old man
crying here
out of the overseer's sight,

pushing his tongue
through where a tooth
would be if he were whole.
the space aches
where his tooth would be,

where his land would be, his
house   his wife   his son
his beautiful daughter.

he wipes his sorrow from
his cheek, then
puts his thirsty finger
to his thirsty tongue
and licks the salt.

i call a name that
could be his.
this offering
is for you old man;
this salty ground,
this gin.

■

jasper   texas   1998

for j. byrd

i am a man's head hunched in the road.
i was chosen to speak by the members
of my body.   the arm as it pulled away
pointed toward me, the hand opened once
and was gone.

why and why and why
should i call a white man brother?
who is the human in this place,
the thing that is dragged or the dragger?
what does my daughter say?

the sun is a blister overhead.
if i were alive i could not bear it.
the townsfolk sing we shall overcome
while hope bleeds slowly from my mouth
into the dirt that covers us all.
i am done with this dust.   i am done.

■

alabama 9/15/63

Have you heard the one about
the shivering lives,
the never to be borne daughters and sons,

the one about Cynthia and Carole and Denise and Addie
Mae?
Have you heard the one about
the four little birds
shattered into skylarks in the white
light of Birmingham?

Have you heard how the skylarks,
known for their music,
swooped into heaven, how the sunday
morning strains shook the piano, how the blast
is still too bright to hear them play?

■

praise song

to my aunt blanche
who rolled from grass to driveway
into the street one sunday morning.
i was ten.   i had never seen
a human woman hurl her basketball
of a body into the traffic of the world.
Praise to the drivers who stopped in time.
Praise to the faith with which she rose
after some moments then slowly walked
sighing back to her family.
Praise to the arms which understood
little or nothing of what it meant
but welcomed her in without judgment,
accepting it all like children might,
like God.

■

august

for laine

what would we give,
my sister,
to roll our weak
and foolish brother

back onto his bed,
to face him with his sins
and blame him
for them?

what would we give
to fuss with him again,
he who clasped his hands
as if in prayer and melted

to our mother?   what
would we give
to smile and staple him
back into our arms,

our honey boy, our sam,
not clean, not sober, not
better than he was, but
oh, at least, alive?

■

study the masters

like my aunt timmie.
it was her iron,
or one like hers,
that smoothed the sheets
the master poet slept on.
home or hotel, what matters is
he lay himself down on her handiwork
and dreamed.   she dreamed too, words:
some cherokee, some masai and some
huge and particular as hope.
if you had heard her
chanting as she ironed
you would understand form and line
and discipline and order and
america.

■

birthday 1999

it is late.   the train
that is coming is
closer.   a woman can hear it
in her fingers, in her knees,
in the space where her uterus
was.   the platform feels
filled with people
but she sees no one else.
she can almost hear the
bright train eye.
she can almost touch the cracked
seat labeled lucille.
someone should be with her.
someone should undress her
stroke her one more time
and the train
keeps coming closer.

it is a dream i am having
more and more and more.

■

grief

begin with the pain
of the grass
that bore the weight
of adam,
his broken rib mending
into eve,

imagine
the original bleeding,
adam moaning
and the lamentation of grass.

from that garden,
through fields of lost
and found, to now, to here,
to grief for the upright
animal, to grief for the
horizontal world.

pause then for the human
animal in its coat
of many colors.   pause
for the myth of america.
pause for the myth
of america.

and pause for the girl
with twelve fingers
who never learned to cry enough
for anything that mattered,

not enough for the fear,
not enough for the loss,
not enough for the history,

not enough
for the disregarded planet.
not enough for the grass.

then end in the garden of regret
with time's bell tolling grief
and pain,
grief for the grass
that is older than adam,
grief for what is born human,
grief for what is not.

■

the gift

there was a woman who hit her head
and ever after she could see the sharp
wing of things   blues and greens
radiating from the body of her sister
her mother   her friends   when she felt

in her eyes the yellow sting
of her mothers dying   she trembled
but did not speak   her bent brain
stilled her tongue so that her life
became flash after flash of silence

bright as flame   she is gone now
her head knocked again against a door
that opened for her only
i saw her last in a plain box smiling
behind her sewn eyes there were hints
of purple and crimson and gold

■

out of body

(mama)

the words
they fade
i sift
toward other languages
you must listen
with your hands
with the twist ends
of your hair
that leaf
pick up
the sharp green stem
try to feel me feel you
i am saying I still love you
i am saying
i am trying to say
i am trying to say
from my mouth
but baby there is no
mouth

■

oh antic God
return to me
my mother in her thirties
leaned across the front porch
the huge pillow of her breasts
pressing against the rail
summoning me in for bed.

I am almost the dead woman's age times two.

I can barely recall her song
the scent of her hands
though her wild hair scratches my dreams
at night.   return to me, oh Lord of then
and now, my mother's calling,
her young voice humming my name.

■

april

bird and bird
over the thawing river
circling   parker
waving his horn
in the air above the osprey's
nest   my child
smiling her I know something
smile   their birthday
is coming   they are trying
to be forty   they will fail
they will fall
each from a different year
into the river   into the bay
into an ocean of marvelous things

■

children

they are right, the poet mother
carries her wolf in her heart,
wailing at pain yet suckling it like
romulus and remus.   this now.
how will I forgive myself
for trying to bear the weight of this
and trying to bear the weight also
of writing the poem
about this?

■

surely i am able to write poems
celebrating grass and how the blue
in the sky can flow green or red
and the waters lean against the
chesapeake shore like a familiar,
poems about nature and landscape
surely   but whenever i begin
"the trees wave their knotted branches
and . . ."   why
is there under that poem always
an other poem?

■

mulberry fields

they thought the field was wasting
and so they gathered the marker rocks and stones and
piled them into a barn   they say that the rocks were shaped
some of them scratched with triangles and other forms   they
must have been trying to invent some new language they say
the rocks went to build that wall there guarding the manor and
some few were used for the state house
crops refused to grow
i say the stones marked an old tongue and it was called eternity
and pointed toward the river   i say that after that collection
no pillow in the big house dreamed   i say that somewhere under
here moulders one called alice whose great grandson is old now
too and refuses to talk about slavery   i say that at the
masters table only one plate is set for supper   i say no seed
can flourish on this ground once planted then forsaken   wild
berries warm a field of bones
bloom how you must i say

■

cancer

the first time the dreaded word
bangs against your eyes so that
you think you must have heard it but
what you know is that the room
is twisting crimson on its hinge
and all the other people there are dolls
watching from their dollhouse chairs

the second time you hear a swoosh as if
your heart has fallen down a well
and shivers in the water there
trying to not drown

the third time and you are so tired
so tired and you nod your head
and smile and walk away from
the angel uniforms the blood
machines and you enter the nearest
movie house and stand in the last aisle
staring at the screen with your living eyes

■

in the mirror

an only breast
leans against her chest wall
mourning   she is suspended
in a sob between t and e and a and r
and the gash ghost of her sister

t and e and a and r

it is pronounced like crying
it is pronounced like
being torn away
it is pronounced like trying to re
member the shape of an unsafe life

■

blood

here in this ordinary house
a girl is pressing a scarf
against her bleeding body
this is happening now

she will continue for over
thirty years emptying and
filling   sistering the moon
on its wild ride

men will march to games and wars
pursuing the bright red scarf
of courage   heroes every moon

some will die   while every moon
blood will enter this ordinary room
this ordinary girl will learn
to live with it

■

walking the blind dog

for wsm

then he walks the blind dog muku
named for the dark of the moon
out to the park where she can smell
the other dogs and hear their
yips their puppy dreams

her one remaining eye is star lit
though it has no sight and
in its bright blue crater
is a vision of the world

old travelers who feel the way from here
to there and back again
who follow through the deep
grass the ruff of breeze
rustling her black coat   his white hair

both of them
poets
trusting the blind road home

■

hands

the snips of finger
fell from the sterile bowl
into my mind and after that
whatever i was taught they would
point toward a different learning
which i followed

i could no more ignore
the totems of my tribe
than i could close my eyes
against the light flaring
behind what has been called
the world

look   hold these regulated hands
against the sky
see how they were born to more
than bone   see how their shadow
steadies what i remain   whole
alive   twelvefingered

■

wind on the st. marys river

january 2002

it is the elders trying to return
sensing the coast is near and they
will soon be home again

they have walked under two oceans
and too many seas
the nap of their silver hair whipping
as the wind sings out to them
this way   this way

and they come rising steadily not
swimming exactly toward shore
toward redemption
but the wind dies down

and they sigh and still and descend
while we watch from our porches
not remembering their names not calling out
Jeremiah   Fanny Lou   Geronimo   but only

white caps on the water   look white caps

∎

the tale the shepherds tell the sheep

that some will rise
above shorn clouds of fleece
and some will feel their bodies break
but most will pass through this
into sweet clover
where all   all will be sheltered safe
until the holy shearing
don't think about the days to come
sweet meat
think of my arms
trust me

■

stop

what you are doing
stop
what you are not doing
stop
what you are seeing
stop
what you are not seeing
stop
what you are hearing
stop
what you are not hearing
stop
what you are believing
stop
what you are not believing

in the green hills
of hemingway
nkosi has died
again
and again
and again

stop

—for Nkosi Johnson
2/4/89—6/1/01

■

aunt jemima

white folks say i remind them
of home   i who have been homeless
all my life except for their
kitchen cabinets

i who have made the best
of everything
pancakes   batter for chicken
my life

the shelf on which i sit
between the flour and cornmeal
is thick with dreams
oh how i long for

my own syrup
rich as blood
my true nephews   my nieces
my kitchen   my family
my home

■

cream of wheat

sometimes at night
we stroll the market aisles
ben and jemima and me   they
walk in front   remembering this and that
i lag behind
trying to remove my chefs cap
wondering about what ever pictured me
then left me personless
Rastus
i read in an old paper
i was called rastus
but no mother ever
gave that to her son   toward dawn
we return to our shelves
our boxes   ben and jemima and me
we pose and smile   i simmer   what
is my name

■

sorrows

who would believe them winged
who would believe they could be

beautiful   who would believe
they could fall so in love with mortals

that they would attach themselves
as scars attach and ride the skin

sometimes we hear them in our dreams
rattling their skulls   clicking

their bony fingers
they have heard me beseeching

as i whispered into my own
cupped hands   enough   not me again

but who can distinguish
one human voice

amid such choruses
of desire

■

this is what i know
my mother went mad
in my fathers house
for want of tenderness

this is what i know
some womens days
are spooned out
in the kitchen of their lives

this is why i know
the gods
are men

■

6/27/06

pittsburgh   you in white
like the ghost
of all my desires   my heart
stopped and renamed itself
i was thirty-six
today i am seventy   my eyes
have dimmed from looking for you
my body has swollen from swallowing
so much love

■

birth-day

today we are possible.

the morning, green and laundry-sweet,
opens itself and we enter
blind and mewling.

everything waits for us:

the snow kingdom
sparkling and silent
in its glacial cap,

the cane fields
shining and sweet
in the sun-drenched south.

as the day arrives
with all its clumsy blessings

what we will become
waits in us like an ache.

■

mother-tongue: the land of nod

true, this isn't paradise
but we come at last to love it

for the sweet hay and the flowers rising,
for the corn lining up row on row,

for the mourning doves who
open the darkness with song,

for warm rains
and forgiving fields,

and for how, each day,
something that loves us

tries to save us.

■

mother-tongue: we are dying

no failure in us
that we can be hurt like this,
that we can be torn.

death is a small stone
from the mountain we were born to.

we put it in a pocket
and carry it with us
to help us find our way home.

■

some points along some of the meridians

heart

spirit path
spirit gate
blue green spirit
little rushing in
utmost source
little storehouse

lung

very great opening
crooked marsh
cloud gate
middle palace

stomach

receive tears
great welcome
people welcome
heavenly pivot
earth motivator
abundant splendor
inner courtyard

liver

walk between
great esteem

happy calm
gate of hope

kidney

bubbling spring
water spring
great mountain stream
deep valley
spirit storehouse
spirit seal
spirit burial ground
chi cottage

large intestine

joining of the valleys
1st interval
2nd interval
heavenly shoulder bone
welcome of a glance

spleen

supreme light
great enveloping
encircling glory
sea of blood
3 yin crossing

gates

stone gate

gate of life
inner frontier gate
outer frontier gate

■

new orleans

when the body floated by me
on the river   it was a baby
body thin and brown
it was not my alexandra
my noah
not even my river
it was a dream
but when i woke i knew
somewhere there is a space
in a grandmother's sleep
if she can sleep
if she is alive
and i want her to know
that the baby is not abandoned
is in grandmothers hearts
and we will remember
forever

■

after the children died she started bathing
only once in a while
started spraying herself with ginger
trying to preserve what remained of her heart

but the body insists on truth.
she did not want to be clean
in such a difficult world
but there were other children

and she would not want me
to tell you this

■

In the middle of the Eye,
not knowing whether to call it
devil or God
I asked how to be brave
and the thunder answered,
"Stand. Accept." so I stood
and I stood and withstood
the fiery sight.

■

Previously Uncollected Poems

"The world has writ the letter now, writ the letter now, 'twas never wrote before."

Lucille Clifton, age 10

All Praises

Praise impossible things
Praise to hot ice
Praise flying fish
Whole numbers
Praise impossible things.
Praise all creation
Praise the presence among us
Of the unfenced Is.

■

bouquet

i have gathered my losses
into a spray of pain;
my parents, my brother,
my husband, my innocence
all clustered together
durable as daisies.
now i add you,
little love, little
flower,
who walked unannounced
into my life
and almost blossomed there.

■

sam, jr.

blood of my mothers blood.
blood of my father
spilling onto the coverlet,
when you are dry this boy
my father watched
running through virginia fields
will be again a dream.
i thought i saw, he said,
a baby boy
running and laughing as he ran
and so i knew that i
would make a son. or break him
brother, and he almost did
but now you smile and bleed
the only blood i share
while i sit watching you run
to our parents there dreamlike
in a field.

■

MOTHER HERE IS MY CHILD

Here is a wreath that skips among the chimneys
flinging flowers
a daughter of the blood.
See she spies the heartsease you blossom
and calls me.
She calls me by your name.
A proper gift,
Sidney among the flowers
adorning you, being by you adorned.

■

Poem To My Yellow Coat

today i mourn my coat.
my old potato.
my yellow mother.
my horse with buttons.
my rind.
today she split her skin
like a snake,
refusing to excuse my back
for being big
for being old
for reaching toward other
cuffs and sleeves.
she cracked like a whip and
fell apart,
my terrible teacher to the end;
to hell with the arms you want
she hissed,
be glad when you're cold
for the arms you have.

■

Poem With Rhyme

i was born yes.
i don't know why.
i have been hated for it,
laughed at,
i have cried, me and my
black yes.
affirmation.
i wonder why i do it,
i can only guess i was
born to it. yes. yes. yes.

■

Rounding the curve near Ellicot City
another raccoon dead, his tail raised high
like a flagpole. Or was she a woman,
striped our sister, trying to reach Oella
which never changes? And did we charge,
my daughters and I, around the bend,
an army of fearless women wrapped in tin?
And does her tail, silent and stiff, signal Danger?
We feel around us, in Ellicot City, the accusation
of a forest of patchy eyes.

■

entering earth

the door is bone
push through
you will be
dressed in blood
rise up
and wobble off
toward cavalry
the ground time here
will be brief
before you remember
your actual name
you will have rattled
back to bone
hover above
the ivory gate
hold your body
in your hands
the ground time here
is brief
drop your framework down
and fly
it has fed you
it will feed your friends

■

to black poets

just cause you don't see me
don't mean i aint there.
when you be together
reading
and being together
and you feel something soft
rubbing you just like sisterskin
don't turn off please,
thats me.

■

quartz lake, Alaska

deep autumn, and all the tourists have gone
south with the geese and fickle sun
only those things remain which can bear
the frown of winter: the ice stars,
the raven, the moon, and this solitude,
keeping their long faith with forsaken things.
the lake turns its cold face,
is no one's mirror,
and the sky pouts back,
everything wakes and sleeps in forest time,
to the soft drum of wind
among the pines, to the snow forever falling and
the long dark bringing its constellations,
bright cruciforms against the sky
lighting the quiet way on snow
for winter migrations of caribou,
or wolf, or phantom grief moving out
and away in a silent
ritual of passage

■

Index of Poems

Titled poems are shown in roman. Untitled poems are indicated by their first line and appear in italics. First lines beginning with *a*, *an*, or *the* are alphabetized under *A* or *T.*

Acknowledgments

It was a great privilege and responsibility to edit this Selected of Lucille Clifton's work. I am immensely grateful to the Cliftons and my editor at BOA, Peter Conners, for trusting me to do this impossible work. I thank both Peter and my partner, Rassan Salandy, for questions they added to my questions and the marveling they added to my marveling.

This book would not be at all without the devotion that is *The Collected Poems of Lucille Clifton* edited by Kevin Young and Michael Glaser. I am ever thankful to them both for carrying such a work into being.

I give thanks to the Rose Library at Emory University, especially Head of Research Services, Courtney Chartier. I thank Ricky Maldonado who sent me recordings of Clifton reading at the 92nd Street Y, one of them from 1969 after she won their Discovery contest. I thank the 11 wonderful thinkers who met with me in a cloud of a room at Pratt where we, around a candle and a packet of materials, thought together about the mysteries and the concrete of Clifton's work. Thank you: Nicole Valdivieso, Ericka Hodges, Tina Zafreen Alam, Jaylen Strong, Dianca London, Jessica Angima, Shayla Lawz, Isa Guzman, Amanda Hohenberg, Charlotte Seebeck, Aliera Zeledon-Morasch. I also thank Andrea Bott, Patty Cottrell, and Beth Loffreda of the Writing Department at Pratt for supporting such a workshop and for coordinating much appreciated photocopying support. My deep thanks especially to Beth Loffreda for the year that helped me to devote such time to this work.

I thank the editors of *Paris Review* for publishing two of the previously uncollected poems: "bouquet" and "Poem To My Yellow Coat." Along with The Estate of Lucille T. Clifton and BOA Editions Ltd., I thank Copper Canyon Press for permission to reprint selections from *The Book of Light* in this volume.

And to these compasses I touch my forehead: Sonia Sanchez, Mendi Lewis Obadike, Cheryl Boyce-Taylor, Ross Gay, Kamilah Aisha Moon. And those who talked with me over the mysterious light of the internet: Eisa Davis, Rachel Eliza Griffiths, Patrick Rosal, Ama Codjoe. They each answered my questions so generously and candidly—with clarity and depth of insight, and with the secret gift of informality, as was the nature of our correspondence. Such exchanges added to my thinking and listening as I made my final selections.

Here is Cheryl Boyce-Taylor about Clifton's work: "Her work appears pure and simple, but man, oh, man. So deadly and deep and honest. She pulls you out of your lies in her work. There's nowhere to tell those lies in your work. You just have to be truthful." And later: "I think her work is political . . . I find her poems open-mouthed just like Sonia."

Here is Eisa Davis: "I think about how truly difficult it must have been (I haven't read her talking about it and perhaps you have) to have written poems about her father violating her. I mean, what did that do? that's emotionally complex and political and fierce for sure.

"I think she had to find a way to keep herself safe, in her mind. so in her poems I feel her drawing a circle around us while smelling a wolf. there's safety to be made, and a leakage of that safety. since the poems are lyrical, especially in the ohs she uses, it's a new gospel I hear . . .she's laughing. a lot. she tells the children to say she's a poet, she don't have no sense—and this means to me that she must have plenty. sense above sense, outside of sense. she writes poems in one movement, about one piece of sense. she survived her father and returned to us as the moon.

"of course that's not all of her work. but then she goes through menopause and cancer and kidney transplant and writes about all that, generously, powerfully, without indulgence . . . she's really the second part of Baraka's 'Fuck poems / and *they are useful* . . .' she's truly showing us how to make it through life."

Here is Kamiliah Aisha Moon on what Clifton's work makes possible: "Permission to be and keep it real. To be shameless, unabashed. To be vulnerable as a show of strength. To wonder and to be amazed. To decipher dreams. To rage eloquently and elegantly. To claim and proclaim." And on the *things* she thinks of in, to borrow from Rita Dove, Clifton's "thingful" work, Moon writes: "Brooms, knife, kitchen counter, bowls, boats. Tools that clear the way, pare; things that allow for making, that carry."

Here is Rachel Eliza Griffiths: "Clifton's work has pushed me away from believing that what is 'simple' is also 'easy,' which is to say, that Clifton has guided me into a tense space of belief, love, and labor. Clifton's faith is chiseled into what is both spoken and unsayable. Her work also asks me to leap and to remember, as Morrison wrote, the natural and earned elements that might be defined as 'freedom.' Clifton's work is the opening in the water and the water, the flight and the brutal symphonic wind the wings make as they lift the body to which they belong. And, too, Clifton's work is a space where the word 'belonging' opens and opens for me. She belongs to herself, to her family, to poetry, to us, and whatever is beyond that. Her work then is also about the autonomy of language, about whom and which words are spared. It is also about whom language, memory, justice do not spare."

Here is Patrick Rosal: "I remember reading 'homage to my hips.' And I think then and throughout my life, that was one of the clearest poems of understanding what the world says you should love and the thing you actually love and care for can be really, really different. And that your own body can be a thing that you care for and love because much of the world doesn't (or doesn't seem to) was something I knew in my experience of being in my own skin and with other folks whom I know were not loved publicly and mythologically. Here was this small poem, also a mythology—of love, acceptance."

Here is Mendi Lewis Obadike on what she learned from Ms. Lucille who was her teacher: "That being a writer has to do with being a part of a community, learning to touch another.

"And poetry is a way of wondering that involves other people."

Here is Ama Codjoe: "Clifton made space for my body in poetry/in the world. My black body. My hips. My histories. My contradictions. My desires. And there are so many mysteries in her writing too. [...] There's more to say but for that I'd want sun spilling through a window, her books around me like a skirt, and you and me with cups and cups of tea."

About the Author

Lucille Clifton (June 27, 1936–February 13, 2010) was an award-winning poet, fiction writer, and author of children's books. Her poetry collection *Blessing the Boats: New & Selected Poems 1988–2000* (BOA, 2000) won the National Book Award for Poetry. In 1988 she became the only author to have two collections selected in the same year as finalists for the Pulitzer Prize, *Good Woman: Poems and a Memoir* (BOA, 1987) and *Next: New Poems* (BOA, 1987). In 1996, her collection *The Terrible Stories* (BOA, 1996) was a finalist for the National Book Award. Among her many other awards and accolades are the Ruth Lilly Poetry Prize, the Frost Medal, and an Emmy Award. In 2013, her posthumously published collection *The Collected Poems of Lucille Clifton 1965–2010*, edited by Kevin Young and Michael Glaser (BOA, 2012), was awarded the Hurston/ Wright Legacy Award for Poetry.

About the Editor

Aracelis Girmay (December 10, 1977) is the author of three books of poems: *the black maria* (BOA, 2016); *Teeth* (Curbstone Press, 2007), winner of a GLCA New Writers Award; and *Kingdom Animalia* (BOA, 2011), the winner of the Isabella Gardner Award and finalist for the National Book Critics Circle Award and the Hurston/Wright Legacy Award. She is also the author/illustrator of the collage-based picture book *changing, changing* and with her sister collaborated on the forthcoming children's book *What Do You Know?* (Enchanted Lion, 2021). For her work, Girmay was nominated for a Neustadt International Prize for Literature in 2018 and in 2015 received the Whiting Award for Poetry. In 2018 she was also selected by Elizabeth Alexander to receive the Lucille Clifton Legacy Award. Girmay is the mother of two and is on the editorial board of the African Poetry Book Fund.

BOA Editions, Ltd. American Poets Continuum Series

253

Colophon

BOA Editions, Ltd., a not-for-profit publisher of poetry and other literary works, fosters readership and appreciation of contemporary literature. By identifying, cultivating, and publishing both new and established poets and selecting authors of unique literary talent, BOA brings high-quality literature to the public. Support for this effort comes from the sale of its publications, grant funding, and private donations.

The publication of this book was made possible by the generous support of the Lannan Foundation and by the special support of the following donors:

Anonymous x4
Reginald Dwayne Betts
Blue Flower Arts, LLC
Angela Bonazinga & Catherine Lewis
Bond, Schoeneck & King, PLLC
Amy Bown
Susan Burke & Bill Leonardi, *in honor of Boo Poulin*
Rick Bursky
Bernadette Weaver Catalana
Chen Chen
Gwen & Gary Conners
Charles & Danielle Coté
The Chris Dahl & Ruth Rowse Charitable Fund
Eliana Dimopoulos
Kevin J. Doherty
Cornelius Eady
JR Fenn & Lytton Smith
Jack & Bonnie Garner
Ross Gay
Robert & Rae Gilson
Alison Granucci
Rachel Eliza Griffiths
Art & Pam Hatton
Kelly Hatton & Tom White
Ellen Hagan
James Long Hale
Kate Harvie
Sandi Henschel, *in memory of Anthony Piccione*
Charlotte & Raul Herrera

Grant Holcomb
Kathleen C. Holcombe
Fred L. Joiner
Jack & Gail Langerak
Peter & Phyllis Makuck
Melanie & Ron Martin-Dent, *in honor of Ron Martin-Dent*
Joe McElveney
Miranda-Tarisa Mims
Roger Mitchell
Kamilah Aisha Moon
Matt Morton
Zohreen Murad
Dorrie Parini & Paul LaFerriere
Boo Poulin
Deborah Ronnen
Salman Rushdie
Steven O. Russell & Phyllis Rifkin-Russell
Matthew Shenoda
Meredith & Adam Smith
Thomas G. Smith
The Steeple Jack Fund
Stephan, Ingmar & Jorden
David St. John
St. John Fisher College Department of English, *in honor of Dr. William Waddell*
Allan & Melanie Ulrich
William Waddell & Linda Rubel
The Wadsworth Family
Eric Warren, *in memory of Vidal Starr Clay*
Michael Waters & Mihaela Moscaliuc
Erica Yunghans